Contents

Italy –
An Overview

With an outline that is instantly recognizable, the country of Italy is made up mainly of a slender, boot-shaped peninsula jutting into the northern Mediterranean, along with two large islands, Sicily and Sardinia. To the north, Italy shares borders with France, Switzerland, Austria and Slovenia. Italy is about the same size as the US state of Arizona. It has a highly successful economy and in 2007 was ranked as the seventh wealthiest economy in the world. Italy's economic strength is partly a result of its strategic position at the centre of Europe. As a member of the European Union (EU), Italy has an economy linked with other EU members, such as France and Germany. In 2002, Italy's adoption of the single European currency (the Euro) led to still closer ties with other EU members that had also adopted the Euro.

OLD AND NEW

Italy is both an ancient country and a fairly young one. Italian culture has influenced the Mediterranean region for many hundreds of years, yet 150 years ago the unified country called Italy did not exist. Two thousand years ago, Italy was home to one of the ancient world's most advanced civilizations, the Roman Empire. Around AD 100, the Romans ruled a vast empire that included many of the lands bordering the Mediterranean Sea.

After the fall of the Roman Empire in the fifth century, Italy was divided into a series of small

▼ Italy's capital, Rome, includes the Vatican City within its borders. St Peter's Square, shown here, is the heart of the Vatican.

city-states (see page 10), often ruled by foreign powers. However, the influence of Italian culture remained strong in Europe and beyond. As the home of the papacy, the city of Rome became the centre of western Christianity. Throughout medieval times, the popes wielded great worldly, as well as spiritual, power (see pages 48-9). During the fourteenth to sixteenth centuries, the region of Italy found itself at the heart of a great artistic awakening known as the Renaissance. Italian painters, sculptors, poets and other artists produced great art treasures and writings (see page 46).

UNIFICATION

In the 1850s, the movement to unify Italy gathered pace. In 1861, the various political regions were brought together as a single country. During the twentieth century, Italy met with mixed fortunes. It sided with Germany during the Second World War and suffered a disastrous defeat. During the 1950s, Italy industrialized rapidly and its economy boomed, though economic progress later slowed.

As citizens of a leading industrial nation, most Italians enjoy a fairly high standard of living. However, a deep divide exists between northern and southern Italy in terms of living standards and resources. The north is wealthy and more industrialized, while the south is poorer and more agricultural. Since the 1950s, successive Italian governments have tried to lessen this divide by spending large sums of money on improving the resources and industries of the south, but with varying degrees of success. In the north, the 1990s saw the rise of political parties campaigning for the region to cut its ties with the south, and become more independent. This campaign gained considerable support among people in the north.

? Did you know?

Two small, independent countries are located inside Italy's borders: the tiny republic of San Marino dating back to AD 301, and the Vatican City inside Rome.

◀ Renaissance Italy produced a wealth of great art treasures. A copy of Michelangelo's sculptural masterpiece, *David*, can be seen standing outside the Palazzo Vecchio in Florence. The original statue is situated inside the Galleria dell'Accademia, also in Florence.

PEOPLE AND LANGUAGE

Around 96 per cent of Italy's people are ethnic Italians (including Sardinians, who view the large island of Sardinia as partly separate from mainland Italy). Small numbers of French, Germans and Slovenes live near Italy's northern borders, with Albanians and Greeks in the south of the country. Italian is a 'Romance' language, derived from Latin and based on a dialect spoken in Tuscany in medieval times. Around the year 1900, only a few of Italy's people spoke what is now standard Italian, the rest spoke regional dialects. Today, dialects are used mainly just by the older generation. Italy's long history as a group of city-states has left Italians with a sense of regional identity which can appear stronger than their sense of national identity. Many people see themselves firstly as belonging to a particular city or region, and secondly as Italian.

ITALY'S REPUTATION

Italy's historic cities, rich culture and sunny climate are world renowned. They attract holidaymakers, and tourism is central to Italy's economy. Italy is also famed as the land of fast cars, high fashion, opera and romance. The national flair for design ensures that Italian clothes, cars and other products sell well abroad. The country is also famous for its cuisine (cooking). Italian-style foods such as pizza, pasta and ice-cream are eaten all over the world.

Italy is also well known for some less positive aspects of its culture. It is notorious as a base for organized crime – especially that of the international criminal organization known as the Mafia, which is involved in the illegal drugs trade. Since the 1990s, Italy has been rocked by a series of scandals, with accusations of bribery, corruption and even violence being levelled at leading politicians and businessmen. Such accusations are still being made today.

Physical geography

- Land area: 294,020 sq km/113,521 sq miles
- Water area: 7,210 sq km/2,784 sq miles
- Total area: 301,230 sq km/116,305 sq miles
- World rank (by area): 70
- Land boundaries: 1,932 km/1,200 miles
- Border countries: Austria, France, Holy See (Vatican City), San Marino, Slovenia, Switzerland
- Coastline: 7,600 km/4,723 miles
- Highest point: Monte Bianco de Courmayeur, secondary peak of Mont Blanc (4,748 m/ 15,577 ft)
- Lowest point: Mediterranean Sea (0 m/0 ft)

NB: all the above data includes Sardinia and Sicily

Source: CIA World Factbook

◄ The Italian diet includes plenty of fresh produce, much of which is grown locally. This stall is selling fresh citrus juices.

Legend

★ Capital

● Cities > 500,000

● Cities > 200,000

• Cities > 100,000

· other cities

▲ Mountain

CHAPTER 2

History

The first settlements in Italy grew up around 4,000 BC, although evidence of human remains have been found dating from 20,000 BC. During the ninth century BC, Phoenicians from the North African city of Carthage colonized southern Italy. Later on, invaders from Greece arrived and claimed much of Italy as part of the Greek Empire. By the seventh century BC, a people called the Etruscans had dominated central Italy and formed an association of twelve city-states, called Etruria.

▼ Public entertainments were staged in amphitheatres like this throughout the Roman world. Gladiator contests, and even re-enactments of sea battles, were staged here at the Colosseum in Rome.

THE ROMAN EMPIRE

According to legend, Rome was founded in 753 BC. In 509 BC, a Latin-speaking people, the Latini, who probably originated north of the Alps, drove the Etruscan king out of Rome and founded the Roman republic. Through a series of wars, the Romans carved out an empire which, by AD 100, stretched from Britain east to Syria, and south into North Africa. The Romans were skilled architects and engineers, and built a network of roads, forts and towns throughout their empire. They constructed aqueducts to carry water, and introduced new farming practices and other innovations that made life easier. Wealthy Romans lived comfortably in town houses or country villas

complete with central heating and sanitation. In large estates and well-to-do households, slaves did much of the work.

Jesus Christ lived and died in the Roman province of Palestine in the Middle East. During the early centuries AD, Christianity took hold in the Roman world, replacing other religions. At first the new religion was outlawed, but in AD 313 the Roman emperor, Constantine, allowed Christians to worship. Rome soon became the base of the papacy (see page 48). In the third century, the Roman Empire was divided in half to make it easier to administrate. The western half was ruled from Rome, the eastern half from Byzantium (later called Constantinople, now Istanbul in Turkey). The Western Empire came under increasing threat from warlike peoples to the north, whom the Romans called Barbarians. In AD 476, the Barbarian leader Odoacer sacked Rome and deposed the last emperor. In the east, the Byzantine Empire remained strong.

? Did you know?

The Romans were responsible for Italy's name. They called the southern part of the country *Italia*, which means 'land where oxen graze'.

Focus on: Vesuvius and Pompeii

In AD 79, the volcano known as Mount Vesuvius near the city of Naples erupted without warning. From a nearby vantage point, the Roman writer Pliny the Younger saw a great cloud of dark ash rise from the mountain and spread across the sky. The cloud of burning ash engulfed the town of Pompeii at the foot of Vesuvius, and all the inhabitants perished. In the eighteenth century, Pompeii was rediscovered and excavated. The thick layer of ash had preserved the town's streets perfectly. Elaborate mosaics and frescos were found intact in wealthy villas. The imprints of the bodies of Pompeii's citizens and even their pets had also been preserved by the ash.

◀ The Roman town of Pompeii is now a major tourist attraction. Streets, buildings and even graffiti on walls have been preserved by the volcanic ash which fell on the town almost two thousand years ago.

Following the breakup of the Western Empire, the geographical region of Italy was divided into a number of smaller territories, many of which became parts of other empires. Meanwhile the popes grew more powerful, and acquired much of central Italy, which became known as the Papal States. Between the ninth and fourteenth centuries, successive popes vied for control of northern Italy. To the north, the Holy Roman Empire ruled much of western Europe. To the south, Byzantium ruled southern Italy and was later succeeded by the Arabs, the Normans and the Spanish.

CITY-STATES AND FOREIGN RULE

The tenth to fourteenth centuries saw the rise of small, independent city-states across much of Italy. Each of these states was centred on a city such as Venice, Genoa, Milan, Florence or Pisa, and governed either by a council of elders or a wealthy merchant or nobleman. City-states such as Milan, Genoa and Venice grew prosperous through trade and banking, and Venice even established an empire of its own. The rulers of Italian city-states were important patrons of the arts, who supported the great artistic flowering of the Renaissance.

Between 1500 and 1800, much of Italy was ruled by foreign powers such as France, Spain and Austria. Following the French Revolution in 1789-92, the French emperor, Napoleon Bonaparte, conquered northern Italy and set up a series of

▼ The Norman rulers of Sicily were great builders, and their architectural influence can be seen in the sweeping lines of this cathedral in Palermo. The Normans employed Arabic craftsmen to decorate the interiors with dazzling mosaics.

republics. After Napoleon's defeat in 1815, Italy was returned to its former state, with the north ruled by Austrians, the south by the Spanish, and the centre by the Papal States. But Napoleon's occupation of Italy had given many of its people a taste for a unified, independent nation. The independent kingdom of Piedmont and the island of Sardinia became a focus for unification.

Did you know?

Around AD 1300, approximately four hundred separate city-states flourished in Italy.

▼ A fifteenth-century woodcut of the port of Genoa. This city-state, a leading centre for trade, was the birthplace of Christopher Columbus.

Focus on: Italian explorers

In medieval times, many great travellers and explorers came from Italy. In the late thirteenth century, a young Venetian, Marco Polo, was one of the first Europeans to visit China. He wrote a famous book about his travels. In 1492, Christopher Columbus, a navigator from Genoa, was commissioned by the Spanish to sail across the Atlantic. His mission was to reach China and the east, but he discovered the 'New World' of the Americas instead. Another Italian explorer, Amerigo Vespucci, gave his name to the Americas. In the fifteenth century, the Venetian navigator Giovanni Caboto, known as John Cabot, explored the coast of Canada.

UNIFICATION AND WORLD WAR

In the 1850s, the *Risorgimento*, or movement to unify the diverse states of Italy, gathered strength. Unification was achieved through three key figures: Giuseppe Mazzini, a political activist, Count Camillo Cavour, chief minister of Piedmont-Sardinia, and Giuseppe Garibaldi, a brilliant soldier. In 1859, Cavour's forces defeated the Austrians in northern Italy.

The army of Piedmont moved south, while Garibaldi invaded Sicily with a force of 1,000 men and swept north. The independent Kingdom of Italy, proclaimed in 1861, was soon enlarged by the addition of Venice and the Papal States.

From the late 1800s, Italy took part in the 'scramble for Africa', when European powers competed to seize African territories. Italy took control of Eritrea, Somalia and Libya. During the First World War, Italy sided with the Allies in an attempt to increase its territory, but did not make substantial gains. In the 1920s, the fascist leader Benito Mussolini rose to power by promising to make Italy a great nation. In 1922, the fascists marched on Rome and the king, Victor Emmanuel III, declared Mussolini as premier of Italy. By 1925, Mussolini had become a dictator, with absolute authority.

In 1936, Italian forces occupied Ethiopia in East Africa. In 1940, Italy entered the Second World War on the side of Nazi Germany, but was defeated by the Allies, who by 1943 had occupied southern Italy. The Italian government surrendered and overthrew Mussolini, but the Nazis took control and installed Mussolini as head of a puppet state in the north. Italy became a war zone, as Allied forces and Italian partisans (resistance fighters opposed to the Nazis) battled their way north up the country. By 1945, Mussolini had been killed and the Allies were victorious.

◀ A statue of Italian national hero Giuseppe Garibaldi. His force of 1,000 volunteers were nicknamed 'redshirts'. In 1860 they conquered Sicily and then Naples.

INTO THE TWENTY-FIRST CENTURY

After the war, much of Italy lay in ruins. However, with the help of the USA, the post-war period brought rapid economic growth and industrialization. In 1957, Italy became a founding member of the European Economic Community (EEC). But in the 1960s Italy's economy slowed and inflation rose (see page 30).

The 1970s brought turmoil, with the rise of right-wing and left-wing terrorist groups opposed to all political parties. Some of these groups carried out bombings, kidnappings and murders. In 1978, a left-wing extremist group called the Red Brigades kidnapped and killed a former prime minister, Aldo Moro. The mid-1980s brought better times, with partial economic recovery and the defeat of terrorism. However, during the 1990s the Italian government was involved in a series of political scandals, with many politicians accused of criminal activities. Italy's attempts to stamp out organized crime and corruption have continued into the twenty-first century (see pages 24-5).

▼ Benito Mussolini (left) and Nazi leader Adolf Hitler watch a parade held when the Italian dictator visited Germany in 1937.

Landscape and Climate

With a land area of 294,020 sq km (113,521 sq miles), Italy is smaller than France, but larger than the United Kingdom. The boot-shaped peninsula of Italy is nowhere more than 170 km (105 miles) wide, but it is 1,200 km (745 miles) long. Italy is surrounded by the seas of the Mediterranean on three sides: the Ligurian Sea to the north-west, the Adriatic to the east, the Tyrrhenian Sea to the west and the Ionian Sea to the south-east.

Italy's coastline stretches 7,600 km (4,723 miles). The 'toe' of Italy lies close to the island of Sicily, the Mediterranean's largest island which covers 25,709 sq km (9,926 sq miles). The rocky island of Sardinia, occupying 24,089 sq km (9,300 sq miles), lies to the west across the Tyrrhenian Sea. In addition, Italy has more than 3,000 smaller islands, such as Elba and Capri.

MOUNTAINS AND LOWLANDS

Much of Italy is covered by uplands. In the far north, the Alps are Italy's highest mountains, rising to 4,748 m (15,577 ft) on the slopes of Mont Blanc, whose summit is in France. The Alps form the national border with France, Switzerland and Austria. East of the Alps rise the Dolomites, a range of craggy limestone peaks. The Apennines form a rugged mountain crest zigzagging down central Italy for some 1,350 km (840 miles).

Lowlands cover less than a quarter of Italy. A large lowland belt lies in the north, sandwiched between the Alps and the

▼ Snow lingers in the Italian Alps late into summer. However, the region's glaciers are shrinking because of global warming.

Apennines. Here the plain of Lombardy in the west merges with the Po valley to the east. This region is extensively farmed and densely populated. Other low-lying plains are found along parts of the west coast and in Puglia, which forms Italy's 'heel'.

Italy's longest river is the Po, which rises in the Alps and flows 652 km (405 miles) to the Adriatic. Other rivers include the Adige, the Tiber and the

? Did you know?

The word 'volcano' comes from the small volcanic island of Vulcano off the coast of southern Italy.

Arno. In the south, some rivers (called *fiumare*) dry up in summer. The large, beautiful lakes of Garda, Maggiore and Como are in the north, with Lake Trasimeno in central Italy.

Italy lies on a geological fault line, a zone of weakness in the earth's crust. Magma (molten rock) surging up through cracks (faults) in the earth's crust produces volcanic eruptions. Italy's volcanoes include Mount Etna on Sicily and the volcanic island of Stromboli. Mount Vesuvius, near Naples, famously erupted in AD 79 (see page 9), and more recently in 1631 and 1944. Some experts believe another eruption of Vesuvius is due.

◄ There are frequent minor eruptions from the crater on Mount Stromboli, on one of the Aeolian islands off the coast of Sicily. Red-hot rocks shoot into the air and fall into the sea with a hissing sound.

Focus on: Where plates collide

Italy is located on a border zone where two of the huge tectonic plates that form the earth's crust meet and push together. Millions of years ago, these same plates, the European and African plates, created the Alps, fold mountains which formed as rock crumpled upwards as the plates

collided. The enormous pressure created by the plate collision also causes rocks to shift, sometimes producing violent earthquakes. Central and southern Italy are particularly prone to earthquakes. The last major earthquake was in 2004 and measured 5.2 on the Richter scale.

CLIMATE

Italy is renowned for its sunny climate, and its skies are mostly clear during spring, summer and autumn. In winter, the skies are often overcast and rainy. In spring, hot, dry air from Africa moves north to cover much of Italy. Summers (June-August) are mainly dry, with occasional thunderstorms. In autumn, cool, moist air moves in from the Atlantic Ocean. Winter (December-February) brings the coolest temperatures.

The height of the land and its closeness to the sea affect local climates, and result in cooler uplands and some milder climates near the coast. Italy's long north-south extent also brings regional variations in climate, which are most obvious in winter. Much of the north has a temperate climate, meaning it is cooler and

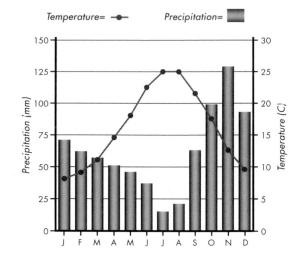

▲ Average monthly climate conditions in Rome

▼ The dry climate means that much of southern Italy is covered by scrubby vegetation. This is the coast around the town of Vietri sul Mare, south of Naples.

wetter than southern areas. The city of Milan experiences average minimum temperatures of 1°C (35°F) in January, while temperatures climb to 28°C (82°F) in summer. Italy's climate becomes progressively hotter and drier further south. Palermo in Sicily has an average January minimum of 8°C (44°F), with temperatures soaring to 30°C (86°F) in summer. Southern Italy is known as the *Mezzogiorno* – the land of the midday sun – because of the scorching heat around noon in summer. Parts of the south and centre are extremely dry, and gripped by drought from time to time.

VEGETATION

Regional differences in climate and terrain suit different types of vegetation, giving rise to a variety of scenery. In the north, the lower slopes of the Alps are clothed in forests of fir and pine, with alpine meadows higher up. Forests of oak,

? Did you know?

The climate of southern and central Italy – hot, dry summers and mild winters – is known as a Mediterranean climate, wherever it occurs worldwide.

beech and pine once covered much of Italy, but these were mostly felled long ago for timber and agriculture. Farming has totally transformed lowland areas like the Po valley, while coastal marshlands have been drained for agriculture. Cypress trees dot the rolling hills of Tuscany in the west. Dense, thorny scrubland called *macchia* covers dry, stony terrain in the south and on Sardinia.

Focus on: Natural disasters

With earthquakes, volcanic eruptions, droughts and floods, Italy has its fair share of natural disasters. In 1908, the port of Messina in Sicily was devastated by a violent earthquake that killed more than 70,000 people. Mount Etna on Sicily is one of Europe's highest active volcanic mountains. Major eruptions occurred here in 1996 and in 2002. In 1994, torrential rains in north-west Italy caused extensive flooding, in which about one hundred people died.

▼ Tall cypress trees frame a farm on a hilltop in Tuscany, providing protection from chill winter winds.

CHAPTER 4

Population and Settlements

In 2008, there were just over 58 million people living in Italy. Between 1850 and 1970, Italy's population rose steeply, but since 1995, the figure has remained almost constant. In the 1950s, the population increased by about 7 per cent each year, but growth fell to less than 4 per cent in the 1980s, and to zero by the mid-1990s. This so-called zero population growth occurs when numbers of births and deaths are equal, and therefore cancel each other out.

By 2005, Italy's population had actually started to fall slightly. Experts predict that this trend will continue over the next decades (see graph). From having a population equal in size to that of France and the UK, Italy's looks set to fall to a similar level to that of Spain today. On average, Italian families have only 1.2 children – fewer than the average of 2.05 children needed to keep the population the same size. There are many reasons for this, including the fact that Italians are marrying later, and that more women are going out to work before and after marriage. Many families want a lifestyle they could not afford if they had more children. In general, family sizes are larger in the south than in the north.

In 2008, around two-thirds of the population were aged between 15 and 64, with only 14 per cent under the age of 15. One fifth of Italians were aged 65 and over, with better healthcare helping people to live longer. This pattern is similar in many European countries. The government fears that, in twenty years' time, not enough adults will be working and paying taxes to support the large numbers of older people who need pensions, increased medical care and other services. Italy's government is now encouraging people to work longer and retire later.

◀ High-rise housing is found in suburbs and in the centres of Italian cities. Modern apartment blocks are a common feature. The apartments shown here were built during the 1960s in a suburban area of Rome.

NORTH AND SOUTH

In 2008, Italy had an average population density of about 193 people per sq km (500 per sq mile). However, the population is not evenly distributed. More people live in fertile lowlands and industrial areas, while mountains and dry areas have fewer people. In the nineteenth and twentieth centuries, a marked contrast developed between northern and southern Italy in terms of population and industrial development. The north became more densely populated, with a climate and terrain favourable for farming, more natural resources and better developed industries. Fewer people lived in the south, with its harsh climate, poor farms and less developed industries.

? *Did you know?*

Many Italians live in *palazzos*. A *palazzo* is not a palace, as the Italian word implies, but an apartment block.

▲ Men enjoy a game of cards at a social club in Sorrento. The proportion of the population aged 65 and over is steadily increasing.

Population data

- Population: 58.1 million
- Population 0-14 yrs: 14%
- Population 15-64 yrs: 66%
- Population 65+ yrs: 20%
- Population growth rate: -0.02%
- Population density: 193 per sq km/499.9 per sq mile
- Urban population: 68%
- Major cities: Milan 2,945,000
    Naples 2,250,000
    Rome 3,339,000

Source: United Nations and World Bank

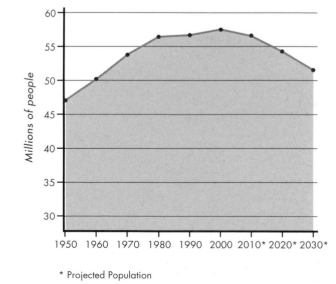

* Projected Population

▲ Population growth, 1950-2030

In the 1950s and 1960s, large numbers of Italians from the south moved to the industrial centres of the north to seek work and a better standard of living. This caused problems such as unemployment and overcrowding in some northern cities, while some villages in the south became deserted. Between 1950 and 1984, the Italian government spent huge sums on the *Cassa per il Mezzogiorno*, a fund to develop the industries, communications and resources of the south. The fund succeeded in areas such as the improvement of transport, but efforts to relocate industry and business met with mixed results. The south still lags behind the north in natural resources, and its climate is less favourable to farming.

ITALIAN CITIES

Just over two-thirds of Italy's population live in urban areas, a figure that has remained roughly constant since 1995. This urban figure is low compared with that of many European countries. From ancient times, settlements grew up in Italy in favoured sites, such as cool hilltops and fertile river valleys, that offered water for irrigation, a means of transport and defence against enemies. Unlike most other countries, Italy is not dominated by a single city. Milan, Rome and Naples are the three largest cities, with over 2 million people each. Turin, Bari, Bologna, Florence, Genoa, Catania, Palermo and Venice are also major conurbations. Each has a distinct character, dating from the days of the city-states. For example, in medieval times, the city of Venice grew wealthy through trade and carved out an empire based on naval supremacy.

◀ The scene in this narrow backstreet in Naples is typical of many cities in southern Italy.

Italian towns are traditionally laid out around one or more squares (*piazze*). Many towns have fine buildings, including churches, dating back to Renaissance, medieval and even Roman times. Older districts have large, handsome houses built around a central courtyard. In modern suburbs, many people live in apartments in high-rise buildings. The poorest housing is often on the outskirts of towns and cities. Although they have great historic interest, Italian cities are not exempt from problems that plague urban areas the world over, including traffic congestion, overcrowding in poor districts, and pollution.

► Every Italian town has at least one *piazza*, although not all are as grand as this one in Amalfi, near Naples.

Focus on: Rome

Rome, 'the eternal city', is Italy's capital and second largest city, after Milan. Its many historic buildings include the Forum, where Romans worshipped and did business, and the Colosseum, where gladiatorial contests were staged. Originally built around seven hills at a crossing on the River Tiber, the city is also known for the underground catacombs where early Christians buried their dead. It is the only city in the world with an independent country inside it – the Vatican. Rome is renowned for its graceful squares and fountains dating from around 1600. In the twentieth century, Rome grew rapidly with the construction of many high-rise offices and apartment blocks. Rome became a thriving centre for finance, trade and industry, including the fashion industry. Modern Rome is a mixture of grand old buildings and modern blocks, with crowded cafés, brightly-lit stores, and noisy traffic winding its way through narrow backstreets.

Government and Politics

In 1946, Italians voted to abolish their country's monarchy and Italy has been a republic ever since. In 1947, the nation's constitution was written to prevent the rise of another dictator like Mussolini. Italy is a parliamentary democracy. Everyone over the age of 18 has the right to vote. The percentage of the population that votes in elections is high compared with many countries. Referendums are sometimes held on major issues such as abortion and electoral reform.

Italy is divided into 20 administrative regions, each of which has a strong identity. All regions have a degree of self-rule and a few, including Sardinia, have considerable autonomy (independence). The regions are subdivided into provinces, and the provinces are divided into units called communes.

ELECTORAL SYSTEM

Italy's parliament, based in Rome, is made up of two houses. Italy's electoral system was reformed in 1993. Seventy-five per cent of members of both houses are directly elected, with the candidate with the most votes in an area winning the seat, and the other parties winning nothing. The remaining 25 per cent of members are elected through the system of proportional representation. With this system, seats are given to parties according to their share of the vote in the whole country. The upper house, or Senate, has 315 members, 232 of whom are directly elected and 83 of whom are elected from the regions by proportional representation. The lower house, the Chamber of Deputies, has 630 members, 475 of whom are directly elected and 155 of whom are elected through the system of proportional representation. Senators and deputies serve a five-year term. There are relatively few women in parliament compared with some European countries.

? Did you know?

Voting is considered a 'civic duty' in Italy. Failure to vote in elections is an offence and can lead to a criminal record.

◀ Pope John Paul II addresses the Chamber of Deputies in 2002. Pope John Paul died in 2005, and was succeeded by Pope Benedict XVI.

The president occupies the largely ceremonial position of head of state. However, in recent years presidents have taken an active role during times of political turmoil, for example, during the *Tangentopoli* scandal (see page 24). Presidents serve a seven-year term. The prime minister, the leader of the most powerful party in government, chooses the cabinet of ministers. Prime ministers do not serve a fixed term and Italy is famous for its frequent changes of prime minister and cabinet. However, many ministers continue to serve in the governments of successive prime ministers, which provides continuity.

▼ The seat of local government – the town hall and main square of Cortona in Tuscany.

POST-WAR POLITICS

Since the Second World War, Italy's complex electoral system has resulted in governments being formed through coalitions, meaning that a number of political parties has shared power. From 1948 to the mid-1990s, the centre-right Christian Democrat Party, with a broadly conservative outlook, dominated Italian politics. The Christian Democrats formed coalitions with other parties, including socialists and liberals, but kept the Communist Party out of government, despite the fact that it had considerable support.

? Did you know?

Since the Second World War, few Italian governments have lasted much more than a year.

Since the 1950s, successive governments have steered Italy's economy while trying to tackle persistent problems, including inflation, unemployment and organized crime in the form of the Mafia (see box opposite). The north-south divide has remained a difficult and lasting issue. During the 1990s, a political party called the *Lega Lombardia* (Northern League) gained considerable support in the north. The League wants the north to become more independent, or even a separate country, and to stop subsidizing the south.

CORRUPTION CHARGES

The early 1990s witnessed a political crisis that changed the face of Italian politics. In 1992, investigations into party finances uncovered a web of bribery and corruption that reached the highest levels of government. Leading businessmen and politicians from every major party were accused of criminal dealings and links with the Mafia. The best known of these was Giulio Andreotti, a leading Christian Democrat who had been prime minister six

times. The scandals were called *Tangentopoli* (*tangente* means bribe and *poli* city in Italian).

Following these scandals, the public lost confidence in existing political parties, and new political alliances were formed. In 1994, the election was won by the centre-right Alliance for Freedom, which included the *Forza Italia* (Come on, Italy) Party, led by Silvio Berlusconi, head of the media empire Fininvest. However, Berlusconi was soon forced to resign following accusations of corruption. His departure enabled the centre-left Olive Tree Alliance to take power in the late 1990s. Despite this, Berlusconi was re-elected in 2001. Another centre-left party, the Union, won in 2006, but in 2008 Silvio Berlusconi claimed victory for the third time.

▼ Former prime minister Giulio Andreotti (centre), was implicated in the *Tangentopoli* scandals of 1992-3. He is seen here after being tried and acquitted on the charge that he protected the Mafia while he was prime minister.

Focus on: The Mafia

The Mafia is a criminal organization with links worldwide, including in the USA. It dates back to medieval times in Sicily, where it grew as a secret organization whose aim was to overthrow foreign rule. Members of the Mafia (*mafiosi*) are bound by a code of silence (*omertà*), which forbids them to betray other *mafiosi*, even rival groups, to the police. By the early twentieth century, the Mafia controlled much of southern Italy. Mussolini almost broke the Mafia's power by imprisoning many of its leaders, but the organization regained strength following the Second World War, when it became increasingly involved in the illegal drugs trade.

Over the years, Mafia members have carried out the assassinations of police officers and judges: killings include those of the Sicilian anti-Mafia judge Giovanni Falcone and his colleague Paolo Borsellino in 1992. In Italy, the Mafia is known as *la piovra*, the octopus, because its tentacles reach everywhere. Nevertheless, public disgust at Mafia killings and threats has been demonstrated more openly in recent times. Since the 1990s, the police have also scored notable successes in arresting a number of Mafia leaders, including Salvatore Riina (arrested in 1993), Leoluca Bagarella (1995), Giovanni Brusca (1996), Vito Vitale (1998) and Mariano Trioa (2006).

▲ In May 1992, a large crowd attends the funeral of murdered judge Giovanni Falcone in Palermo, Sicily, to show support for his anti-Mafia stance.

CHAPTER 5

Energy and Resources

Italy's natural resources include minerals, forests, farmland, and fish in the surrounding waters. However, resources for energy are fairly scarce, and this has restricted the growth of industry and profits from manufacturing.

ENERGY RESOURCES AND USE

Italy has limited reserves of fossil fuels, including oil, natural gas and lignite coal. Oil and natural gas are pumped in the Po valley, Calabria, Sicily, and offshore in the south. Nuclear power provides a relatively small amount of the country's energy. This form of energy is mainly undeveloped following a 1987 referendum in which Italians voted overwhelming against the construction of more nuclear plants. Public opposition to nuclear power deepened following an accident in 1986 at the Chernobyl nuclear reactor in Ukraine. In terms of renewable energy sources, Italy's hydro-electric (HEP) potential is well developed. Hydro-electric plants in the Alps and the Apennines harness the energy of fast-flowing streams to provide power for cities and industry. One of the world's first geothermal plants was built at Larderello. Here, cold water pumped underground is heated by volcanic rocks and used to produce steam, which drives turbines to generate electricity. Use of solar power is limited at present but, with Italy's sunny climate, this form of energy has considerable potential. Italy has one of the fastest growing wind sectors in the world, and wind and wave power could be utilized more extensively in future.

In 2001, Italy consumed 1.7 per cent of all the energy used worldwide. Nearly one-third of this was used in transport, with homes consuming around another quarter and industry a third. Italy's limited energy sources do not meet its power needs. Some 75 per cent of the energy it uses is imported, mostly in the form of oil and natural gas. The nation's power plants burn mainly oil imported from Libya, Iran and other oil-producing nations.

◀ In mountainous parts of Italy, hydro-electric plants are used to generate electricity. Around 17 per cent of Italy's electricity is produced by HEP.

Energy data

- Energy consumption as % of world total: 1.7%
- Energy consumption by sector (% of total),
Industry:	31.7
Transportation:	32.2
Agriculture:	2.4
Services:	3.5
Residential:	26.9
Other:	3.3
- CO_2 emissions as % of world total: 1.6
- CO_2 emissions per capita in tonnes p.a.: 7.8

Source: World Resources Institute

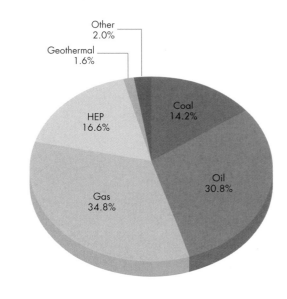

▲ Electricity production by type

Focus on: Carrara marble

The town of Carrara in the Apennines in Tuscany produces top quality marble for use in construction and sculpture. Mining began here in Roman times. Marble, a hard, attractively veined rock, is metamorphic, which means it forms when limestone is subjected to great heat and pressure underground. In Renaissance times, the sculptor Michelangelo came here to choose the marble he required for his magnificent sculptures. He carved his masterpiece, the statue of David, from a block of Carrara marble that had been botched and left abandoned by another sculptor. Carrara marble, which polishes to a smooth, shiny finish, is still prized by sculptors today.

◄ Large blocks of finest marble stand ready for transport at a quarry in Carrara. The marble is traditionally used in sculpture, but it is also in demand in the construction industry.

▲ Salt is extracted from seawater at this plant near Bari. Water is allowed to flood shallow lakes, like this one. The water evaporates, leaving salt, which is raked into heaps.

MINERALS

Italy's stocks of minerals are also fairly scarce. Sicily, Sardinia, Tuscany, Lombardy and Piedmont are the chief mining areas. Iron ore, mercury, potash, zinc, lead, feldspar, pumice and barite are mined commercially. Pyrite, from volcanic areas in the south, is used in the chemical industry and to produce fertilizer and matches. The quarries of Carrara in Tuscany are famous for their marble (see page 27). Elsewhere in the country, granite is quarried. Salt is extracted from seawater on the Adriatic coast near Bari. With scant mineral reserves, Italy must import large quantities of iron ore and other materials it needs for industry.

FISHING, FORESTS AND FARMLAND

The long coastline is excellent for fishing, a traditional industry in Italy. The waters of the Adriatic and the shallow seas off Sicily provide the best fishing grounds. Tuna, sardines, swordfish and anchovies are among the main species caught commercially. In recent decades, long, floating drift nets have been set to catch fish that swim close to the surface. These nets have proved so efficient that stocks of fish have fallen sharply. The authorities have had to introduce quotas to control the number of fish that can be caught. Shellfish such as shrimps and mussels are also caught, as are squid and octopus. Fish and shellfish catches are consumed locally by Italians and by tourists. They are also canned or otherwise processed for sale abroad. Fish and shellfish have been reared in shallow lagoons along Italy's coast since Roman times. Today, the main species farmed commercially is the Mediterranean mussel.

After many centuries of felling, there is little forest left in Italy. The largest surviving forests grow in Abruzzi in central Italy, and Calabria and Puglia in the south. Native species in these forests include holm oak, beech and Aleppo and Corsican pines.

Some 53 per cent of Italy is used for agriculture: 15 per cent is pasture, while 38 per cent is arable. This farmland includes 26,980 sq km (10,520 sq miles) of irrigated land. The largest tracts of farmland lie in the north. Here, in the Lombardy plain and the Po valley, wheat, grapes, olives and sugar beet are grown. Beef and dairy cattle, pigs, chickens and sheep are also raised in many parts of Italy. However, Italy does not produce sufficient meat to meet its needs, and must import the rest, for example, beef from Argentina. The dry climate, poor, stony soil and steep terrain of the south hinder farming, but sheep and goats are pastured here. Durum (hard) wheat for pasta is also grown in the south. Terracing on the steep hillsides helps to prevent erosion.

? Did you know?

In Sicily, in an annual event called the *mattanza*, fishermen spread their nets in the shallows to catch large, meaty tuna as they arrive to spawn.

▼ Harvesting durum wheat in fields near Foggia in Puglia. This type of hard wheat is used to make pasta, a staple food of Italy.

Economy and Income

Since the 1950s, Italy has seen a major shift from a largely agricultural to a highly industrialized economy. During the 1950s, Italy's economy grew rapidly, but it slowed during the 1960s. However the economy has grown in the last few years, and economic growth is now at 1.5%. In 2007, Italy had a workforce of 24.71 million, with unemployment estimated at 6%, and the country ranked seventh in the world in terms of Gross National Income (GNI).

Italy is a leading producer of vehicles, clothing, machinery, iron and steel, chemicals, processed foods and ceramics. One reason for Italy's economic success since the Second World War has been its ability to combine new technology with a flair for design across a wide range of manufactured goods, from cars and computers to clothing and kettles.

WORKING CONDITIONS

Many Italian companies are small, family-run businesses employing fewer than one hundred

Focus on: FIAT

The car manufacturer, FIAT, is one of Italy's most successful companies and a major employer. It was founded in 1899, at the dawn of the motor car age. Based in Turin, the company now has factories elsewhere in Italy and in 50 countries worldwide. FIAT also owns vehicle manufacturers Lancia, Ferrari, Alfa Romeo and Masserati, which operate under their own names. In addition to cars, trucks and tractors, FIAT also makes aircraft engines, telecommunications equipment and heart pacemakers and is involved in insurance, property and publishing – owning one of Italy's best-selling newspapers, *La Stampa*. In 2007, the FIAT Group employed 77,679 people in Italy.

? Did you know?

FIAT stands for *Fabbrica Italiana Automobile Torino* – the Italian Automobile Factory of Turin.

◀ Ports such as Castellammare di Stabia in the Bay of Naples have extensive shipyards. These were developed by the French occupiers in the eighteenth century and have been in use ever since.

people. However, there are also large companies, many of which are part-owned by the government. These include banks, steelworks, shipyards and car factories. In the second half of the twentieth century, the percentage of women in the workforce rose steadily, with large numbers of women working within service industries, but fewer working in industry. Wages are relatively low compared with other European nations – this is another reason why Italy has the edge over some of its competitors.

Unions are traditionally strong in Italy. Workers pay high taxes, but working conditions are generally good and pensions generous. However, a number of small businesses operate within the 'hidden economy'; this means they fail to register and thus avoid paying taxes. These businesses tend to pay low wages. Despite attempts to equalize industry and job opportunities throughout Italy, wages in the south lag behind those of the north, and there is higher unemployment in the south than there is in the north.

SERVICE INDUSTRIES AND AGRICULTURE

Service industries are the most important sector of the economy, employing 63 per cent of all workers and producing 69 per cent of the GNI in 2004. The service sector includes jobs in government, trade, finance, transport and social services. Retailing and hotels and restaurants, boosted by tourism, are a major money-earner. The tourist industry is geared towards foreign and Italian holidaymakers (see pages 52-3).

▲ Tourism is an important earner in beautiful areas such as the island of Capri. Boat excursions are popular in many resorts.

Economic data

- Gross National Income (GNI) in US$: 1,991,284,000,000
- World rank by GNI: 7
- GNI per capita in US$: 33,540
- World rank by GNI per capita: 30
- Economic growth: 1.5%

Source: World Bank

During the 1950s, around 33 per cent of all Italy's workers were involved in agriculture. By 2007, only 5 per cent of workers were employed in agriculture, which produced just 3 per cent of the GNI. Italy's main crops include wheat, maize, rice, sugar beet, olives, and grapes for winemaking. Many regions of Italy are known for their wines, with climate and soil suiting different grapes. Italy is the world's leading producer of tomatoes and tomato products. Fruits and vegetables grown here include cherries, apples, peaches, oranges, potatoes, soya beans and globe artichokes.

INDUSTRY AND MANUFACTURING

In 2007, industry (including manufacturing, construction and mining) employed 32 per cent of workers and yielded 28 per cent of the GNI. Despite the government's attempt to kick-start manufacturing in the south, Italy's industrial heartland remains the north, particularly in and around the cities of Turin,

Milan and Genoa. Craft industries producing leather goods, glass and ceramics date back to medieval times, and different cities are known for characteristic products: leather from Naples, jewellery from Florence, and glass from the island of Murano in Venice.

Italy is a leader in the world of fashion, including clothing, shoes, perfume and accessories (see box opposite). Since the 1950s, top manufacturers have employed cutting-edge designers to create stylish but highly functional goods, including furniture and tableware. Italy is also a top vehicle manufacturer, with FIAT known for family cars (see page 30), Ferrari, Alfa Romeo and Lamborghini for sports and racing cars, Vespa for scooters and Ducati for motorbikes. Italy also produces aircraft and vehicle parts, including tyres by Pirelli. Electronic goods, such as computers, are manufactured in Italy (notably by Olivetti). Zanussi, Delonghi and others produce domestic appliances, such as refrigerators, cookers and washing machines.

◄ Many Italians prefer to buy fruit and vegetables from market stalls or small, family-run grocery shops rather than large supermarket chains. This greengrocer's shop is in Sorrento.

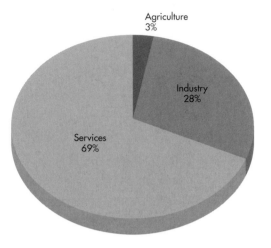

Agriculture
3%

Industry
28%

Services
69%

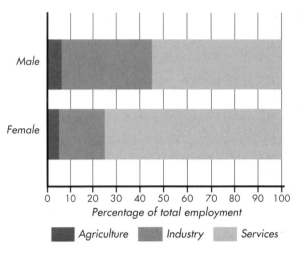

Male

Female

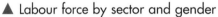

0 10 20 30 40 50 60 70 80 90 100
Percentage of total employment

■ Agriculture   ■ Industry   ■ Services

▲ Contribution by sector to national income

▲ Labour force by sector and gender

Focus on: Fashion

Italy is one of the world's fashion capitals, with names such as Gucci, Armani, Prada, Versace and Benetton known internationally. The fashion industry is mainly based in Milan. Italian people have a reputation for being very fashion conscious, with northerners in particular known for their love of designer clothes. Benetton began as a small, family-run business in 1965, and now owns a chain of shops worldwide. The house of Armani, founded in 1975, produces designer clothing, as well as perfume and accessories. Twice yearly the fashion houses launch their new collections on the catwalks of Milan, Paris, London and New York.

◀ Top models show off the latest collection by Italian designer Donatella Versace at a fashion show in Milan.

CHAPTER 8

Global Connections

From medieval times, Italian city-states forged links with other European nations through trade and finance. Further links were political: parts of Italy became colonies of foreign nations such as France, Austria and Spain. In the early 1900s, Italy itself colonized Somalia, Eritrea, Libya and later Ethiopia. This forged new connections, some of which still influence modern trade patterns, for example, Libya supplies Italy with oil.

ECONOMIC AND POLITICAL TIES

In 1957, Italy was among the six founding members of the European Economic Community (EEC). The EEC's main purpose was to ease trade among its European members by removing import and export duties. In 1992,

the EEC was renamed the European Union (EU) and had 15 member states. By 2007 it had expanded twice, and had 27 member states. In addition to enjoying free trade, EU members work for closer political ties. However, to date, Italy, along with most other EU countries, has stopped short of adopting the European constitution, which would represent a further step on the road to union.

EU money has helped to regenerate industry in southern Italy, for example, by providing grants for poor farmers. As EU citizens, Italians are now free to work anywhere within the EU. In 2002, Italy abandoned its national currency, the

▼ Goods are unloaded from a bulk cargo vessel at Salerno port, a major cargo port for southern Italy.

lira, in favour of the single European currency, the Euro. Many Italians believe that economic targets set by the EU have forced Italian governments to take a more disciplined approach to the economy. This has helped to keep inflation and interest rates low. However, the Euro is not popular with everyone in Italy (partly because prices rose when the Euro was adopted), and recently there have been calls to bring back the lira.

Italy is a member of many other international organizations besides the EU. They include the United Nations (UN) and NATO (the North Atlantic Treaty Organization). In the early 2000s, Italy has worked closely with other UN and NATO members to maintain international peace and security following the rise of Islamic terrorism and the bombing of the World Trade Center in New York City on 11 September 2001.

▲ Italian troops were among the forces involved in the war in Iraq in 2003. Here two Italian soldiers walk in front of a military police base that has been destroyed in a suicide bomb attack.

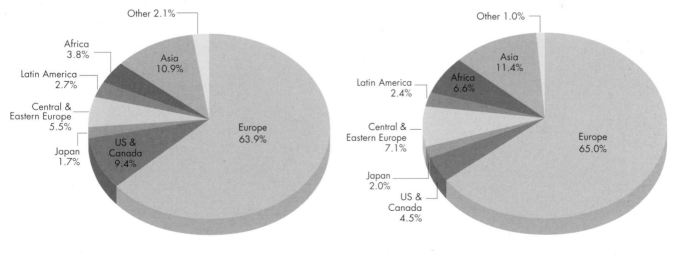

Other 2.1%
Africa 3.8%
Latin America 2.7%
Central & Eastern Europe 5.5%
Japan 1.7%
US & Canada 9.4%
Asia 10.9%
Europe 63.9%

Other 1.0%
Latin America 2.4%
Central & Eastern Europe 7.1%
Japan 2.0%
US & Canada 4.5%
Asia 11.4%
Africa 6.6%
Europe 65.0%

▲ Destination of exports by major trading region

▲ Origin of imports by major trading region

▲ The Italian obsession with coffee is legendary, and over the years Italian habits and customs – and coffee-shops – have travelled to many parts of the world, including here in South Korea.

TRADING PARTNERS

Much of Italy's trade is done within Europe, with 63.9 per cent of exports and 65 per cent of imports passing to and from other EU members. Trade with the USA is also important. Italy's main exports are machinery and equipment, clothing, shoes, vehicles, chemicals, food and drink. Italy's chief imports are machinery, oil, vehicles, chemicals, minerals and food, which chiefly come from Germany, France, the UK, the Netherlands and the USA.

Since the 1980s, Italy has spent more on its imports than it has made from its exports, resulting in a trade deficit (shortfall). The shortfall has also been caused by the rising price of oil, which is imported to provide energy. Foreign currency from the tourist industry helps to offset the imbalance.

Italian trade connections include those of the Mafia, which has unofficial links with other nations, smuggling and trafficking in illegal drugs. In recent years, the Italian government has tried to crack down on the 'informal sector', which can involve all sorts of activities, from unlicensed but otherwise legal street trading to international drugs trafficking. The taxes raised from bringing legal informal businesses within the formal sector would make a substantial contribution to the economy.

? Did you know?

Between 1861 and 1973, some 26 million Italians emigrated abroad.

EMIGRATION AND IMMIGRATION

Since the unification of Italy in the 1860s, millions of Italians have emigrated to other countries, including Germany, Switzerland and the Americas. Italians, especially from the south, have left in search of work and a better life. The early 1900s saw a huge number of Italian emigrants settling in US cities such as New York and Boston, and in Latin American countries such as Argentina and Brazil. Emigration peaked in the 1950s and 1960s, with 390,000 leaving in 1961 alone.

The early 1970s saw a shift, with more immigrants arriving in Italy than emigrants leaving the country. Some of the arrivals were Italians returning home having made money abroad. Others were from Eastern Europe and North Africa, where living standards were lower than in Italy. Like other nations, Italy sets quotas to limit the number of immigrants entering the country legally. However, many refugees from nations bordering the Mediterranean take advantage of Italy's long coastline to enter illegally. In 1990-1 and again in 1997, waves of Albanian refugees fled to Italy to escape political crisis or war, and 1992 saw a flood of refugees from the former Yugoslavia, fleeing war.

◀ Italian-American communities in the USA celebrate traditional Catholic feast days. Here Italian-Americans in Manhattan celebrate the festival of San Gennaro.

Focus on: Italian-American communities

New York, Boston and many other US cities have Italian neighbourhoods. These are the legacy of the early 1900s, when large numbers of Italians arrived to begin a new life in the USA. Such neighbourhoods have stores selling Italian foods, and there are Italian societies, and Catholic church services held in Italian. Original (or first-generation) Italian immigrants spoke little English, but their children were taught English at school. Third- and fourth-generation Italians may speak very little Italian, and only their surnames reveal their origins.

Transport and Communications

Italy's long, narrow shape and mountainous terrain present difficulties for land travel. Sicily, Sardinia and the smaller islands are, of course, isolated by sea. Nevertheless, Italy's transport and communications networks are well developed and generally efficient. Between the 1950s and mid-1980s, the *Cassa per il Mezzogiorno* (see page 20) improved transport and communications in the south.

ROAD AND RAIL

Italy's 484,688 km (301,172 miles) of roads are all paved, and include 6,529 km (4,057 miles) of *autostrada* – motorway. Between 1955 and 1975, a major road-building programme was carried out largely by private companies, so road users are charged tolls on certain roads, for example, motorways. Routes such as the Simplon Pass and the Mont Blanc tunnel cut through the Alps, and link Italy with France, Switzerland and Austria to the north, while the *Autostrada del Sol* (Highway of the Sun) links northern and southern Italy.

? Did you know?

In 1924, Italy began building the world's first toll motor highway. The highway linked Milan with Varese to the north.

▼ High-speed trains provide fast connections between certain Italian cities, for example, Milan and Rome.

With about one in every two Italians a car-owner, city roads are congested during rush hours. Flyovers ease congestion, while noisy scooters and small cars navigate narrow streets. Many people travel to work or school by public transport – either by bus, train, coach or tram, or by metro in Rome and Milan.

Italian railways are state owned, subsidized and inexpensive to use. There are frequent services, and many people consider this the best way to travel about Italy. The rail network includes around 19,460 km (12,092 miles) of track, of which some 12,000 km are electrified. Under Mussolini, the network was improved and magnificent stations, such as Milan, were built. High-speed trains can cover the 1,320 km (819 miles) from Milan to Reggio di Calabria at the tip of Italy in 11 hours. However, Italian trains are notorious for their lack of punctuality, and many journeys involve long delays.

AIR AND WATER TRANSPORT

Historically, the sea offered an effective means of travel between coastal cities. Although it is not as speedy as travel overland, sea transportation is still used extensively in Italy today. Italy has fifteen major seaports, including Genoa, Trieste, Naples, Bari, and Augusta in Sicily. Many oil tankers dock at either Genoa or at Porto Foxi in Sardinia, while La Spezia in the north-west is mainly a container port.

▶ Electric buses provide efficient inner-city transport in centres such as Naples, shown here.

Transport & communications data

- Total roads: 484,688 km/301,172 miles
- Total paved roads: 484,688 km/301,172 miles
- Total unpaved roads: 0 km/0 miles
- Total railways: 19,460 km/12,092 miles
- Airports: 132
- Cars per 1,000 people: 667
- Mobile phones per 1,000 people: 1,230
- Personal computers per 1,000 people: 367
- Internet users per 1,000 people: 496

Source: World Bank and CIA World Factbook

Ferries and hydrofoils link the mainland with offshore islands and with France, Greece and Turkey. The Po is the only major navigable river, with canals leading to the northern lakes. The only means of travel within the city of Venice is by water (see box below).

Air travel is the quickest way of covering long distances on the Italian peninsula. Of the 132 airports listed in 2008, over one hundred have paved runways. All major cities have airports, with many operating international flights.

Leonard da Vinci airport at Fiumicino, near Rome, and Linate and Malpensa, near Milan, are the busiest airports. The national airline, Alitalia, is largely government owned.

COMMUNICATIONS AND MEDIA

Italy has highly developed communications systems, with fast, fully automated telephone, fax and data services. In 2005, there were 25 million land telephones. Mobile phone use has risen rapidly since 1995, when only a small

Focus on: Transport in Venice

With no roads, railway or metro in Venice, the only way to get about is by boat or on foot. This famous city was founded in the fifth century and lies just offshore in the north-east of the country. It is made up of 117 islands, linked by 400 bridges, and was originally built on wooden stilts driven into the mud. Venice's 'streets' are 150 canals. People travel about the city centre by *vaporetto* (waterbus) or *motoscafo* (launch). Venice's famous gondolas offer expensive tourist rides, but specific types of gondola are also used to collect rubbish, deliver goods and for funerals.

◀ Gondolas and other boat traffic dock at piers like this one in Venice. This view of the Church of Santa Maria della Salute is a favourite with artists and photographers.

percentage of Italians had mobiles; now there is more than one mobile phone per person. Internet use is also increasing quickly, although the number of Internet hosts, 4.1 million in 2007, is not high for a nation with advanced technology. Although only one in three Italians owned a personal computer in 2006, almost half of the population used the Internet.

Italy's state broadcasting company, RAI, has three channels which tend to represent different political viewpoints. Silvio Berlusconi's media empire, Fininvest, operates three further channels, including the popular Canale 5. In addition to three state-run radio stations, there are thousands of local and privately owned stations. Half of all Italians own a TV, and there is one radio per person. There are some seventy daily newspapers, owned either by political parties, the Church or large businesses, and

many of them therefore offer a particular political outlook. The most popular daily newspapers are Rome's *La Repubblica*, Milan's *Corriere della Sera*, and Turin's *La Stampa*. There are also numerous magazines, mostly dedicated to particular interests, such as sport and fashion.

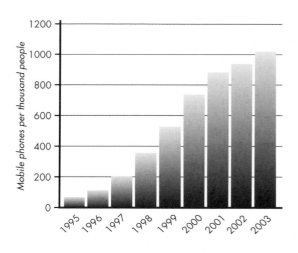

▲ Mobile phone use, 1995 2003

Focus on: Pioneers of telecommunications

In the early days of telecommunications, Italians led the way with many pioneering inventions. In the 1850s, Giovanni Caselli invented the *pantelegrafo*, a device that was a forerunner of modern fax machines. In 1871, Antonio Meucci designed an early telephone; however, later in the decade, Scottish-born Alexander Graham Bell patented the invention. Guglielmo Marconi was a pioneer of radio who sent the first radio signals across the Atlantic from Newfoundland to Britain.

◀ Mobile phones are popular particularly with younger people in Italy, as elsewhere in the world.

CHAPTER 10

Education and Health

Education and, particularly, health are high priorities in Italy. In 2004, Italy spent 4.7 per cent of its Gross Domestic Product (GDP) on education. It spent 8.7 per cent of its GDP on health – a proportion higher than that of the UK, but lower than that of the USA.

Some 98 per cent of Italians over the age of 15 can read and write. Literacy is slightly higher among men than women, reflecting past attitudes to gender and schooling. In the past, more boys than girls continued in secondary education, but this is no longer the case.

PRIMARY AND SECONDARY EDUCATION

In Italy, education is free and compulsory for all children between the ages of six and 14. Many children go to nursery school between the ages of three and five. Ninety per cent of children go to state-run schools. Compulsory schooling is split into five years of primary education and three years of middle school (*scuola media*). This may be followed by four or five years of optional senior secondary education, which can take the form of study at a technical or teacher-training school, or an arts- or science-orientated course at a *liceo*, or college. Italy's education system is currently being overhauled to bring it into line with other EU countries. This will extend the age of free, compulsory schooling to 16. In 2006, 99 per cent of children attended primary school and 94 per cent attended secondary school. Forty-one per cent of students continued their studies at college or university.

▼ A lesson in progress in a class at a primary school in Rome.

Class sizes are small in Italy; there was one teacher for every 11 primary school pupils in 2006. The school day is fairly short, with classes from 8-8.30 am to 1.30-2 pm. The school year runs from September to June. Pupils who gain poor results must repeat a year before continuing with their education. This affects about 11 per cent of girls, but more than 20 per cent of boys.

HIGHER EDUCATION

Senior secondary school graduates may attend university, but some courses are so popular that would-be students must take an entrance exam.

Italy has 45 public universities, of which Rome is the largest with over 170,000 students. There are also private universities, many of which are run by the Catholic Church. University enrolment has risen steadily since the 1960s, with 1.25 million students now in higher education each year.

? Did you know?

The University of Bologna in north-central Italy is among the world's oldest universities, dating from the eleventh century.

Focus on: The national curriculum

Italy has introduced a national curriculum, to standardize education across the country and ensure all students are well prepared for exams. The government's Ministry of Education is responsible for setting educational priorities and selecting coursework books. Middle school pupils study geography, mathematics, science, history and civic education, Italian, art, and a foreign language. Senior secondary school students follow an arts, classics, language or science-based course, or major in vocational training (for example, teacher training).

Education and health

- Life expectancy at birth male: 77.1
- Life expectancy at birth female: 83.2
- Infant mortality rate per 1,000: 6
- Under five mortality rate per 1,000: 4
- Physicians per 1,000 people: 4
- Health expenditure as % of GDP: 8.7%
- Education expenditure as % of GDP: 4.7%
- Primary net enrolment: 99%
- Pupil-teacher ratio, primary: 11
- Adult literacy as % age 15+: 98

Source: United Nations Agencies and World Bank

◄ Chinese students at Bologna University – one of Europe's oldest centres of learning.

University tuition fees are quite low, but students do not receive grants for living expenses. Many students remain at home with their parents to avoid paying rent. They work part-time to cover their living expenses, which means they take longer to complete their degrees. Since the 1960s, the number of women in higher education has risen steadily, but unemployment is higher among female graduates than it is among males.

HEALTH

Standards of medical care in Italy are generally good. The national health plan provides low-cost medical care for all citizens. With one doctor for every 270 patients, Italy has a high doctor to patient ratio. Most Italians eat a healthy diet, with plenty of fresh fruit and vegetables. Pasta is central to the Italian diet.

In general, Italians eat fewer processed foods that are high in fat and sugar than people in many other western countries.

Infant mortality is low in Italy, with just six deaths for every 1,000 live births in 2008. The death rate for children under five is also low, with four deaths for every 1,000. Life expectancy at birth rose steadily in Italy in the late twentieth century, as a result of improvements in public health and sanitation and continuing advances in medical science. In 1960, the average life expectancy at birth was 69.1 years, rising to 73.9 in 1980, and to 80 in 2008. As is the case elsewhere in the world,

▼ A doctor attends an elderly patient at his home in Basilicata, a poor part of the south.

women live somewhat longer than men. Average life expectancy in 2008 was 83.2 years for women and 77.1 years for men.

As people live longer, the increasing number of older people puts more and more pressure on Italy's health system. Changes are being made to cope with the growing demand from older people. Traditionally, older people were looked after by their families, but this is changing as more women are in paid employment, working outside the home.

The major causes of death in Italy are cancer and heart disease. In 2008 there were an estimated 10.6 deaths for every 1,000 people – similar to other nations in Western Europe. The number of deaths per thousand actually

rose slightly in the 1990s, but has since fallen again. HIV/AIDS affected an estimated 0.5 per cent of the population in 2005, with an estimated 400 deaths from AIDS in 2007.

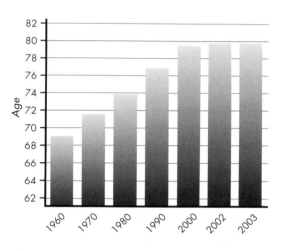

▲ Life expectancy at birth, 1960-2003

▲ The Italian diet consists of a relatively healthy balance of fresh foods, including meat, which provides protein, and carbohydrates such as pasta and bread. Italians also eat lots of fresh vegetables and salads.

Culture and Religion

Italy is internationally renowned for its great artistic achievements, particularly dating from the Renaissance, but continuing into modern times. As the home of the pope, it is the spiritual heartland of Roman Catholics throughout the world.

ART AND LITERATURE

The word 'renaissance' means 'rebirth'. During the Renaissance, from the fourteenth to sixteenth centuries, classical arts and learning were revived and new art forms evolved. Great Renaissance artists include Giotto (lived around 1267-1337), Sandro Botticelli (1444-1510) and Raphael (1483-1520). Michelangelo (1475-1564) was a Florentine sculptor, painter, architect and poet. His sculpture, *David*, and his frescos in the Sistine Chapel in Rome are masterpieces of the depiction of the human form. Michelangelo's contemporary, Leonardo da Vinci (1452-1519), produced one of the world's most famous images, the *Mona Lisa*. Leonardo was also a great scientist and engineer. Some of Italy's best-known literary figures also date from Renaissance times. The poets Dante, Petrarch and Giovanni Boccaccio all produced great works, including the epic poem *The Divine Comedy* (by Dante), which describes a journey through hell and purgatory to heaven, and *The Decameron* (by Boccaccio), a collection of short stories.

The Baroque period followed the Renaissance and saw the work of painter, architect and sculptor, Giovanni Lorenzo Bernini (1598-1680), and dramatic religious paintings and portraits by the Venetian artist Titian (1490-1576).

The twentieth century produced new, dynamic art movements, including Futurism and, in the 1960s, the Art of the Poor. Twentieth-century Italian poets include Salvatore Quasimodo (1901-68), while modern novelists include Dario Fo, Primo Levi and Umberto Eco, who wrote the novel *The Name of the Rose*.

◄ Some modern Italian artists draw inspiration from the landscape, while others produce abstract or conceptual art. This artist is working on a classic Italian street scene in Sorrento.

MUSIC

Italians are justly proud of their musical heritage. Early composers, such as Giovanni Palestrina (lived around 1525-94), Claudio Monteverdi (around 1567-1643) and Antonio Vivaldi (around 1678-1741), wrote beautiful church music. The nineteenth century was the golden age of Italian opera, with Gioacchino Rossini (1792-1868), Gaetano Donizetti (1797-1848), Giuseppe Verdi (1813-1901) and Giacomo Puccini (1858-1924) all composing great works. Every major Italian city has an opera house – La Scala in Milan is the most famous. During the latter part of the twentieth century, the tenor singer, Luciano Pavarotti, helped to revive interest in opera worldwide.

Italy is also renowned for filmmaking. An important and influential era of Italian filmmaking was neo-realism, which refers to a period during the 1940s when directors such as Luchino Visconti, Vittorio De Sica and Roberto Rossellini made films working in real locations and using local people as well as professional actors. Films such as *Ossessione* (Visconti), *The Bicycle Thieves* (De Sica) and *Stromboli* (Rossellini) focused on human problems in natural settings. In the 1960s, 'spaghetti Westerns' (so-called because they were Italian-made) caught the public imagination. Italian filmmaker Sergio Leone directed three films, beginning with *For a Fistful of Dollars*, which made an international star of US actor Clint Eastwood. Acclaimed Italian film directors of more recent times include Bernardo Bertolucci (*The Last Emperor*) and Roberto Benigni (*The Postman* and *Life is Beautiful*).

Did you know?

The terms commonly used in written music are Italian, for example, *piano* (soft), *forte* (loud), *lento* (slow), *andante* (moderate walking pace) and *con brio* (lively).

▼ The audience settles down for an opera performance at the Roman amphitheatre in Verona.

RELIGION

In 1985, a public referendum decided that Roman Catholicism was no longer to be Italy's state religion; nevertheless, it is still the dominant faith. In 2004, 79.9 per cent of Italians were Roman Catholics and some 1.2 per cent followed Islam (most Muslims were immigrants from North and West Africa). Another 2.3 per cent followed other religions, including Protestantism and Judaism. The remaining 16.6 per cent stated they had no religion.

Despite official statistics, the number of practising Catholics is falling in Italy. Some 97 per cent of Italians are baptized, but only about one in three of this group attends church services regularly. Some sources put this figure as low as one in ten. The number of young people entering religious orders has also fallen steeply. However, the parish priest remains a respected member of the community, especially in rural areas, where faith is often stronger than in the cities.

In the past, the Catholic Church exerted great influence on social values in Italy. However, the Church's influence in the country has waned in recent decades. Catholic doctrine opposes abortion, divorce and artificial methods of birth control. However, in 1970 the Italian government voted to permit divorce and, in a 1978 referendum, Italians voted to legalize abortion. The low birth rate suggests that most people in Italy practise birth control.

Focus on: The Vatican City

The Vatican City, occupying less than 0.5 sq km (0.2 sq miles) in Rome, is the headquarters of the Catholic Church, which has over 850 million followers worldwide. This tiny, independent state has its own diplomatic corps and security force (the Swiss Guard) with 120 men. Rome has been Catholicism's base ever since St Peter, the first pope, was buried there in ancient times.

◀ A view from the roof of St Peter's Basilica over the Vatican City and Rome. The Vatican houses masterpieces by Renaissance artists such as Raphael and Michelangelo.

◄ The south is the stronghold of Catholicism in Italy. Here the people of Calabria celebrate the feast of the Virgin Mary with a procession.

FESTIVALS

The Church's influence is still strong in terms of tradition and festivals. Most national holidays are Catholic feast days. In addition to Christmas and Easter, these include Epiphany, All Saints' Day, the Assumption and the Immaculate Conception. These last two honour the Virgin Mary. Easter is preceded by Lent, a period of fasting that lasts 40 days during which, traditionally, meat is not eaten. The word carnival comes from the Italian *carne vale*, meaning 'meat, farewell'. Just before Lent, carnivals in Rome, Venice and elsewhere are held, with people parading through the streets wearing masks and costumes.

In addition to national festivals, every town and village has its own patron saint, with feast days marked with processions and celebrations. Some of these festivities incorporate customs dating back to medieval or even Roman times. The city of Siena is home to a twice-yearly horse race held to honour the Virgin Mary. Riders in medieval costume race bareback around Siena's main square.

THE VATICAN

In the eighth century, the Frankish king, Charlemagne, gave a huge tract of land to the pope, and this formed the basis of the Papal States. In addition to this vast territory, popes also wielded immense spiritual and political influence throughout medieval times and beyond. During the 1860s, the papacy opposed Italy's unification, and the Papal States were the last region to become part of Italy in 1870. After this, popes retreated to the Vatican. In 1929, under Mussolini, the Lateral Treaty formalized relations between Church and state, and the Vatican became an independent country. In 2005, Pope Benedict XVI became the 264th successor to St Peter.

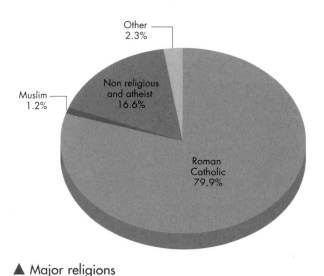

Other
2.3%

Muslim
1.2%

Non religious and atheist
16.6%

Roman Catholic
79.9%

▲ Major religions

CHAPTER 12

Leisure and Tourism

With four to six weeks' paid holiday a year, Italians have more time off than workers in many countries. The warm, sunny climate allows Italians to make the most of their leisure time. It also makes Italy a popular destination for foreign tourists.

FAMILY CUSTOMS

The family lies at the heart of Italian culture and everyday life. Traditionally, elderly people have tended to live with their grown-up children and grandchildren. However, this practice is becoming less common, especially in big cities where life is less traditional than in rural areas. In Italian culture, the mother and son are the focus of the family. Many sons remain at home until they reach their thirties, with their mothers attending to their every need. However, when men marry, they may find that their wives are less willing to perform this role since they also go out to work. Popular songs are written in praise of mothers, and Italians even have a name for their national devotion to the idea of the mother, *mammismo*.

FOOD

Italian mothers have a reputation for being wonderful cooks, and Italians generally are passionate about food, as are the many visitors who sample real Italian cooking. Italian food is one of the world's most popular cuisines. One of the country's most famous dishes, pizza, is usually eaten as a light meal, followed by a dessert of ice cream, one of Italy's most famous inventions. Italians are renowned for their love

▼ Pizza is baked in an oven in the kitchen of a modern restaurant in Vico Equense near Naples. In many restaurants, pizza is still baked in traditional brick-lined ovens.

of coffee, with many different types including *espresso*, *cappuccino* and *caffelatte*. Pasta, made from wheat, comes in many shapes and sizes, including spirals, shells, curls and ribbons, and of course, *spaghetti*, which means 'little strings'.

Italians usually buy their ingredients fresh from the many excellent markets. Shops open in the morning and early evening, and close between 1pm and 4pm to avoid the hottest part of the day. The main meal, traditionally enjoyed at midday, is now generally eaten in the evening. It consists of several courses, of which *antipasti* or appetisers, such as cooked meats or salad, are the first. Next is a course of pasta, soup or risotto, followed by the main dish of meat or fish, accompanied or followed by vegetables.

Then comes cheese and/or fresh fruit and dessert. All this may be washed down with a fine Italian wine.

LEISURE ACTIVITIES

Italy's mild climate means that people spend much of their leisure time outdoors, perhaps enjoying a game of *bocce* (bowls) or a drink in the local café. The evening stroll, or *passeggiata*, provides a chance to gossip with friends and show off new clothes. In towns and cities, Italians enjoy evening concerts and plays, and people from all walks of life (not merely the rich) attend the opera. Italians are also keen cinemagoers, although in recent decades television has caused a drop-off in cinema attendances.

? Did you know?

Pasta did not originate in Italy. The Venetian merchant and traveller, Marco Polo, brought it back from China to Italy during the thirteenth century.

▼ Onlookers watch the world go by during the evening *passeggiata* in the coastal resort of Sabaudia, not far from Rome.

SPORT

Italy is a nation of sports enthusiasts. Italians love both watching and playing sport and football is often said to be a national obsession. Milan, Turin and Rome have two major league teams apiece: Milan is home to AC and Intermilan, Turin is the base for Torino and Juventus, and Roma and Lazio are located in Rome. The national team, nicknamed the *azzurri* (blues), arouses great enthusiasm. Italy has won the World Cup four times, most recently in Germany in 2006.

Cycling has a big following, with the key race, the *Giro d'Italia* (Tour of Italy) taking place in May or June. Italy has two Formula 1 circuits, and motor racing is popular (Italy is a leading manufacturer of racing cars). Basketball, volleyball and baseball are played, along with watersports, such as swimming, rowing and yachting. Italians also enjoy skiing and snowboarding in the mountains.

HOLIDAYS AND TOURISM

Most Italians take at least two weeks of their annual holiday in summer – usually in August. At this time, many shops and factories in inland cities close, and traffic jams occur during the mass exodus and return. Over 80 per cent of Italians holiday within their own country, heading for the coast or mountains, for example, the Alps. However, foreign tourism is becoming increasingly popular and more than 25 million Italians travelled abroad as tourists in 2006.

Tourism is an important industry in Italy, bringing in 8.1 per cent of foreign earnings in 2006. Tourism also provides employment, although many jobs in hotels, restaurants and shops are only seasonal. The number of foreign tourists visiting Italy rose in the late 1990s, peaked in 2000 and has dropped off slightly since then. Nearly half of all foreign visitors head for Venice, and nearly a quarter visit the major historic cities of Venice, Florence and Rome.

◄ In summer, the Italian mountains are a magnet for coach tours, and for more active visitors such as hikers, climbers and mountain-bikers.

◀ The famous leaning tower of Pisa is now in danger of collapse. Conservation efforts are focused on shoring up the unstable ground on which the tower is built.

Among the many attractions are art galleries such as the Uffizi in Florence, and historic sites dating from ancient or Renaissance times, including the Roman town of Pompeii near Naples, the Greek temples in Sicily, and the great cathedrals. Coastal resorts such as Portofino in the north-west, Rimini on the Adriatic and Amalfi and Capri further south are popular with Italians and foreigners. While vital to the economy, tourism also causes problems, including congestion and pollution. Uncontrolled development has spoiled some stretches of the Italian coast.

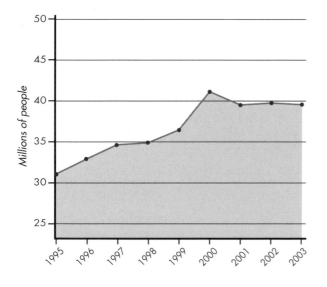

▲ Changes in international tourism, 1990-2003

Tourism in Italy

- 🗁 Tourist arrivals, millions: 41,058,000
- 🗁 Earnings from tourism in US$: 41,644,000,000
- 🗁 Tourism as % foreign earnings: 8.1
- 🗁 Tourist departures, millions: 25,697,000
- 🗁 Expenditure on tourism in US$: 27,437,000,000

Source: World Bank

? *Did you know?*

The Leaning Tower of Pisa is a major tourist attraction. Subsidence caused the tower to lean soon after construction began in 1173.

CHAPTER 13

Environment and Conservation

Land, air and water pollution are all problems in Italy, especially in densely populated and highly industrialized areas. Wild habitats are disappearing, and, although national parks help to protect the nation's wildlife, some of this is under threat.

AIR AND WATER POLLUTION

In built-up areas, exhaust from traffic and emissions from industry cause air pollution. Cities such as Bologna and Milan have closed some of their central areas to traffic in an effort to curb pollution and congestion, while Naples and Florence have introduced buses that run on cleaner fuels, such as LPG. Waste gases from cars, cities and power stations also mix with water vapour in the air to produce acid rain, which damages historic buildings.

Acid rain also kills trees and wildlife in lakes and rivers and is a particular problem in the northern industrial areas. Since the 1980s, the government has introduced laws to curb the release of waste gases.

As a highly industrialized nation, Italy burns large amounts of fossil fuel, and so adds to the release of carbon dioxide (CO_2) and other gases that contribute towards global warming. Warming weather worldwide is causing sea levels to rise, which in future may threaten low-lying cities such as Venice (see box opposite). Italy has signed the Kyoto Protocol, an

▼ This electric car, made by the Italian company Start Lab, helps to improve urban environments. Its small size eases congestion and parking difficulties.

international agreement to reduce CO_2 emissions, and the government has set targets for reducing emissions.

Italy's rivers and surrounding seas are polluted by waste from towns, factories and agriculture. The Mediterranean is one of the world's most polluted seas, and the Adriatic is one of the worst affected areas. Pesticides and fertilizers used in farming run off the land into rivers such as the Po and discharge into coastal waters, causing algae (microscopic plants) to multiply. This so-called algae bloom reduces oxygen levels in the water, harming aquatic life; it is also unsightly and smelly, which puts off tourists. Italy is party to several treaties to restrict the dumping of waste at sea, but agricultural run-off is difficult to regulate.

Focus on: Venice in peril

The city of Venice is under threat. Its historic buildings are slowly but surely sinking into the lagoon on which the city is sited. Pollutants in seawater are eating away at foundations, and buildings are also damaged by the waves caused by passing boats. In winter, when very high tides occur, seawater floods parts of the city, including St Mark's Square with its ancient and beautiful buildings. The worst floods have struck in 1979, 1986 and 2001. Many solutions have been proposed, of which the most practical may be to build a barrage (barrier) across the lagoon entrances, to protect against very high tides.

▲ Tourists wade barefoot across a flooded St Mark's Square in Venice after autumn rains and high tides caused the water level of the Venetian lagoon to rise.

THREATS TO LAND AND SOIL

In past years, Italy disposed of huge amounts of domestic waste in pits called landfill sites. Now a shortage of such sites is causing a crisis in waste disposal here, as elsewhere in Europe. The Italian government encourages recycling to reduce the amount of waste. Italy's record on recycling is one of the best in the world. Around half of all used paper and glass is recycled.

Over the last 2,000 years, most of the ancient forests that once covered Italy have been felled. Without the roots of trees and other plants to

▼ An Italian woman recycles used glass bottles at a bank in Naples. Recycling centres like this one are now in use all over Italy.

keep the soil in place, the land quickly becomes eroded. Deforestation and overgrazing by livestock have led to erosion on steep hillsides. In 1996, a landslide into the Bay of Naples damaged property and killed five people. One way to tackle erosion is to plant more trees. Much of the 23 per cent of Italy that is covered by forests has been fairly recently planted. Another way to limit erosion is to reduce the number of livestock grazing in steep areas.

In general, wetlands absorb moisture and so help prevent flooding. The draining of wetlands to create new land for industry and farming has increased the risk of floods in Italy. In 1966, priceless artworks in Florence were ruined when the River Arno burst its banks. The worst floods in recent decades struck Piedmont and Liguria in 1994.

WILDLIFE AND CONSERVATION

Italy's spectacular wildlife includes golden eagles, bears, wolves and lynx in remote mountains, and wild boar and mouflon sheep (a type of wild mountain sheep) on Sardinia. However, Italian wildlife is under threat for several reasons, of which habitat loss is the most important. Over the centuries, grasslands, forests, marshes and even remote uplands have been cleared to make way for new farms, industrial sites, roads and suburbs. Very little natural vegetation is left in areas such as the Po valley.

Mammals such as deer and boar are threatened by the Italians' enthusiasm for hunting, as are songbirds. The hunting lobby is a powerful force in politics. In a 1990 referendum it won the vote against a ban on hunting. On the positive side, laws are now in place to protect endangered species such as wolves, bears and boar. The setting up of reserves and national parks has helped to preserve some rare species. Italy has about 20 national parks, some of which date from the 1920s, and more are planned. Alpine parks such as Stelvio and Gran Paradiso protect chamois (a type of goat antelope), ibex (a type of wild goat) and marmots (ground squirrels), while mouflon sheep and boar roam in Sardinian reserves.

Environmental and conservation data

- Forested area as % total land area: 33.9
- Protected area as % total land area: 7.2
- Number of protected areas: 643

SPECIES DIVERSITY

Category	Known species	Threatened species
Mammals	132	12
Breeding birds	478	15
Reptiles	55	4
Amphibians	45	5
Fish	168	17
Plants	5,599	3

Source: World Resources Institute

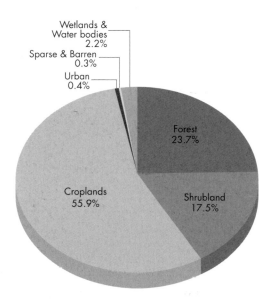

Wetlands & Water bodies 2.2%
Sparse & Barren 0.3%
Urban 0.4%
Forest 23.7%
Croplands 55.9%
Shrubland 17.5%

▲ Habitat type as percentage of total area

? Did you know?

Stelvio in the Alps of Lombardy is Italy's largest national park, covering 1,350 sq km (521 sq miles).

◀ Pony trekking offers an environmentally friendly way to see the landscape in Abruzzo National Park.

CHAPTER 14

Future Challenges

Italy entered the twenty-first century as a dynamic, prosperous nation with a well-developed economy. Italy's generous welfare system means that most of its people enjoy a good quality of life. However, persistent problems remain, including sluggish economic growth, organized crime and the divide between north and south.

DIVISIONS WITHIN ITALY

Despite the funds spent on the south since the 1950s, the country still divides into a prosperous north and a welfare dependent south with high unemployment. Much has been done to generate industry and improve the infrastructure in the south, but natural disadvantages remain. The government cannot change the harsh southern climate, which makes farming difficult, nor can it remedy the scarcity of resources. Future governments will need to try to continue supporting the south while placating the northern leagues – a difficult balancing act.

The political scandals of the 1990s caused a major shake-up in Italian politics but did little to reduce the country's bureaucracy, which stifles political and economic reform. Recent prime ministers have been elected on a pledge to root out organized crime and the Mafia. Yet the Mafia's octopus-like tentacles continue to reach all levels of Italian society.

▼ The wealth of the north is reflected in this affluent shopping centre in Milan.

◀ Poverty is still a persistent problem in many parts of the south, including on the island of Sardinia. Poorer people, including members of ethnic minorities such as Roma (Gypsy) people, shown here, often struggle to survive.

WELFARE AND THE ECONOMY

Many analysts predict that Italy's population will fall within the next few decades. If current trends continue, the population may drop from 58 million to around 54 million by 2050. The growing numbers of older people will place an increasing burden on the state in terms of pensions, medical care and other benefits. The government recently reduced its financial commitments by changing the rules on pensions, including those of government employees. State employees used to be able to retire after 25 years' employment. This has been raised to 35 years, with a retirement age of 57. Meanwhile, to help pay for its welfare system, the government could gain additional contributions towards its Gross National Product if it were to succeed in levying taxes from those who operate within the informal or 'hidden' economy (see page 36).

Since the late 1950s, Italy has been at the forefront of European politics. Many Italians believe the European Union has had a positive effect on the country's economy, helping to tighten monetary policy and stimulate new growth. Many Italians look to the EU to lessen unemployment and keep inflation rates low. In recent decades, Italy has struggled with its balance of payments, with monies spent on imports exceeding the revenue from exports. Future governments will continue the effort to stimulate economic growth while considering the needs of the environment – another delicate balancing act.

? Did you know?

Italy currently spends about 10 per cent of its Gross National Product on pensions – more than double the amount it spends on education.

Timeline

800-900 BC The Phoenicians colonize parts of southern Italy.

700-800 BC The Greeks found colonies in southern Italy.

600-700 BC The Etruscan civilization reaches its height in central Italy.

509 BC Etruscans are driven out of Rome by a Latin-speaking tribe, and Rome becomes a republic.

27 BC-AD 14 Augustus rules as the first Roman emperor.

AD 79 The eruption of Vesuvius destroys the Roman town of Pompeii.

117 The Roman Empire reaches its greatest extent, under the Emperor Trajan.

264 The start of the reign of Emperor Diocletian, during which the Roman Empire is divided into eastern and western halves.

330 Emperor Constantine moves capital of Roman Empire to Byzantium (now Istanbul).

476 Barbarian leader Odoacer sacks Rome and deposes the last western Roman emperor. The eastern branch, the Byzantine Empire, remains intact.

800 Land given to the pope by the Frankish king, Charlemagne, forms the basis of the Papal States. Charlemagne is crowned emperor of the Romans by the pope. This allegiance forms the basis for the Holy Roman Empire.

800-1100 Holy Roman emperors vie with successive popes for control of northern Italy. This rivalry allows for the emergence of the Italian city-states.

1000s The Normans colonize Sicily and southern Italy.

1265 The French become rulers of Sicily.

1300-1550 The age of the Renaissance.

c.1520-50 Spain and the Holy Roman Empire defeat France to control much of Italy.

1707 Austrian rulers take control of northern Italy.

1797 The French emperor, Napoleon Bonaparte, invades northern Italy, bringing the ideals of the French Revolution. He founds several republics.

1815 Napoleon is defeated, and Italy is returned to its former rulers, which include Austria and Spain.

1859-60 Piedmontese forces under Count Cavour defeat the Austrians in northern Italy and head south. Garibaldi and a force of 1,000 soldiers land in Sicily and move north to meet the Piedmontese army at Teano.

1861 The kingdom of Italy is proclaimed under the ruler of Piedmont-Sardinia, King Victor Emanuel II.

1866 Venice becomes part of the kingdom of Italy.

1870 The Papal States become part of Italy.

1908 A major earthquake strikes the port of Messina in Sicily, killing at least 70,000 people.

1911 Italy seizes Libya in North Africa.

1915-18 Italy sides with the Allies (Britain, France and Russia) during the First World War.

1922 Fascist leader Benito Mussolini becomes prime minister.

1925 Mussolini becomes dictator of all Italy.

1936 Italy seizes control of Ethiopia.

1940 Under Mussolini, Italy enters the Second World War on the side of Germany.

1945 War in Europe ends in victory for the Allies.

1946 Italy votes to abolish the monarchy and become a republic.

1948 Italy's new constitution comes into effect. Christian Democrats form the first of many coalition governments.

1950s Italy industrializes rapidly.

1950-1984 Italian governments fund the *Cassa per il Mezzogiorno* to develop the south.

1957 Italy becomes one of six nations to found the European Economic Community (EEC), which later becomes the European Union (EU).

1966 The River Arno floods in Florence, damaging art treasures. Venice also floods.

1970 Divorce is made legal in Italy.

1973-1980 The rise of terrorism in Italy by both right- and left-wing extremist groups.

1978 The Red Brigades kidnap and assassinate ex-prime minister Aldo Moro. Italians vote to make abortion legal. The election of a Polish cardinal as Pope John Paul II breaks with four hundred years of tradition, during which all popes have been Italian.

1980 An earthquake in Campania in southern Italy kills more than 4,500 people.

1983 Bettino Craxi becomes Italy's first socialist prime minister.

1985 Roman Catholicism is no longer Italy's state religion.

1987 A mass trial of Mafia suspects in Palermo results in 338 convictions.

1990 The political party called the Northern League emerges, calling for northern Italy to become independent of the south.

1992 Sicilian judge Giovanni Falcone is killed by a Mafia car bomb.

1992-3 The *Tangentopoli* political scandals bring about the downfall of many leading politicians and existing parties, such as the Christian Democrats. Birth of new political alliances.

1992 The EEC becomes the European Union (EU) with fifteen members.

1994 A coalition including *Forza Italia* led by Silvio Berlusconi takes power. However, Berlusconi resigns following accusations of corruption later the same year.

1994 Floods in north-west Italy kill more than one hundred people.

1996 The Olive Tree Alliance takes power in Italy.

2001 Silvio Berlusconi is re-elected prime minister.

2002 Italy adopts the single European currency.

2004 The EU expands to 25 members.

2005 Pope Benedict XVI became the 264th successor to St Peter.

September 2005 Italy seeks help from the EU to deal with the large numbers of illegal immigrants attempting to enter the country.

April 2006 A centre-left coalition led by Romano Prodi takes power after the narrowest of political victories.

Glossary

Allies The name given to the combined forces fighting against the German side during the First and Second World Wars. In the First World War, Britain, France, Italy and Russia and the USA fought against Germany, Austria-Hungary and Turkey. In the Second World War, Britain, France, the USA and the Soviet Union were allied against Germany, Italy and Japan.

Coalition A government formed by an alliance between several political parties.

Communist Party A political party advocating communism, a system of government in which power resides with a single party which controls all economic activity and provides services.

Conservative Having an outlook that opposes rapid change. In party politics, a right-wing party that supports private ownership.

Constitution A set of laws governing a country or organization.

Democracy A political system in which members of parliament are chosen by people voting in free elections.

Depose To overthrow.

Developed countries The richer countries of the world, whose industries are well-developed, including the USA, many European nations and Japan.

Dictator A ruler with absolute (complete) authority.

Erosion The wearing away of the land by natural forces, such as wind, rain and ice. Erosion is sometimes caused by deforestation.

Exodus A mass departure.

Fascist In politics, a party that favours strict government control of labour and industry. Power is often concentrated in the hands of a strong leader in fascist parties.

Fossil fuel Coal, oil, gas and other fuels formed from fossilized remains of plants or animals that lived millions of years ago.

Frankish Of or relating to the Franks, a Germanic nation that conquered France in the sixth century.

Fresco A mural painting in which the pigment (paint) is applied directly to wet plaster.

Geothermal energy Energy from hot rocks located underground.

Global warming Rising temperatures worldwide, caused by the increase of carbon dioxide and other gases in the atmosphere that trap the sun's heat.

Industrialization The process of developing a country's industries and manufacturing.

Inflation A general increase in prices within a country.

Infrastructure The facilities needed for a country to function, including communications and transport.

Internet host Internet site often representing an organization and ending in .com, .net or .org.

Irrigation The artificial watering of land in order to grow crops.

Liberal In general, tolerant or generous. Also describes political parties that support democratic reform and the abolition of privilege.

Literacy The ability to read and write.

North Atlantic Treaty Organization (NATO) A military alliance formed between the USA and several European countries following the Second World War. The aim of the alliance was to prevent a Soviet invasion of Europe.

Papacy The office of the pope, head of the Roman Catholic Church.

Papal Of, or belonging to, the pope.

Partisan A member of the Italian resistance during the Second World War, opposed to the Nazi Party and Mussolini.

Pollutant A substance that dirties the air, water or land when released.

Proportional representation A system of electing members of parliament by giving seats to political parties according to their share of the vote in the whole country

Puppet state A state that is controlled by another, but with a nominal ruler who has little real power.

Quota A share allotted by agreement to a particular organization or country.

Reactor Part of a nuclear power plant where energy is made by splitting atoms.

Referendum A public vote on a single issue.

Republic A nation state without a monarch, ruled by the people or their representatives.

Risorgimento The movement to unify Italy in the 1800s; 'Resurrection' in Italian.

Sewage Dirty water from homes and factories, containing chemicals and human waste.

Tectonic plate One of the giant rigid sections that make up the earth's outer layer or crust.

Socialist Describes a person, or a political movement that favours a system of government in which a nation's wealth and infrastructure belong to all its citizens, not just to private individuals.

Subsidence When the ground level sinks.

Toll Fee charged for using a road or other transport link.

Turbine Machine powered by steam, gas or water that is used to generate electricity.

United Nations (UN) An organization founded at the end of the Second World War with the aim of preventing future wars. Today more than 150 nations belong to the UN.

Further Information

BOOKS TO READ

Countries of the World: Italy
Sally Garrington
(Evans Brothers, 2004)

Country Files: Italy
Ian Graham
(Franklin Watts, 2006)

Countrywise: Italy and Italian
Emma Sanstone
(Chrysalis Children's Books, 2003)

What's it Like to Live in: Italy?
Jillian Powell
(Wayland, 2007)

Rome (Alpha Holy Cities)
Nicola Barber
(Evans Brothers, 2003)

Heinemann Advanced History:
Italian Unification 1820-71
Martin Collier
(Heinemann Educational, 2003)

Letters From Around the World: Italy
Fiona Tankard
(Cherrytree Books, 2002)

The Changing Face of: Italy
Kathryn Britton
(Wayland, 2007)

Living in: Italy
Ruth Thomson
(Franklin Watts, 2005)

FICTION

Escape from Pompeii
Christina Balit
(Frances Lincoln Children's Books, 2005)

The Name of the Rose (Vintage Classics)
Umberto Eco
(Vintage, paperback reissued 2004)

USEFUL WEBSITES

http://www.italyontheweb.org
Italy on the web, an official site providing information about Italy.

http://www.italiantouristboard.co.uk/it/index.html
Italian State Tourist Board site for the UK.

www.cia.gov/library/publications/the-world-factbook/geos/it.html
The CIA World Factbook, providing up-to-date statistics on Italy.

http://www.infoplease.com/ipa/A0107658.html
Information about Italy's geography, economy, government and people.

http://en.comuni-italiani.it/
Information and statistics on Italian regions, provinces and cities.

Index

Page numbers in **bold** indicate pictures.

About the Author

Dr Jen Green received a doctorate from the University of Sussex (Department of English and American Studies) in 1982. She worked in publishing for 15 years and is now a full-time writer who has written more than 150 books for children. She lives in Sussex.

ENGLISH

Author

Frank Fitzsimons

CONTENTS

WHAT YOU NEED TO KNOW ABOUT ENGLISH AT GCSE

It is important to know what is expected of you. This page shows how your course is structured, how to begin your revision and where you can find ideas for catch-up assignments.

HOW YOUR COURSE IS ORGANISED

The **course-work** requirement accounts for **40%** of your final grade: 20% for speaking and listening and 20% for **reading and writing.**

SPEAKING AND LISTENING
(EN1 = SPEAKING AND LISTENING)
Three **orals:**

A single   A paired   A group

The marks are added up and then divided by three for the final mark. It is worth doing as many orals as you can. The best in each category can then be submitted as your mark.

READING (EN2 = READING)
You can read a wide range of **Shakespeare plays** but the play you will read will probably depend on what is available in the English stock cupboard. It is worth remembering that the Shakespeare assignment is also counted as part of the GCSE in English Literature.

- **Wide Reading (EN2 = Reading)**
This is a **comparison** of two texts in which you will be assessed on your reading. One of the texts must have been written before 1914 by an author recognised within The National Curriculum. This assignment also forms an **important part** of the course-work for GCSE Literature.

- **Media (EN2/3 = Reading/Writing)**
This assignment can range from a comparative analysis of two soap operas from different countries to an analysis of an advert. The media assignment is considered as both a **reading** and a **writing** assignment.

WRITING (EN3 = WRITING)
- **Original and Personal Writing**
This is creative writing where you may write a story or a number of poems.

- **Personal Writing**
This includes non-fiction writing that can be discursive (about anything). However, you need to be aware that work-placement diaries are not now expected of the more able candidates!

EXAMS ACCOUNT FOR 60% OF YOUR GRADE

READING (EN2)
- **Prepared texts:** two groups of texts (poems or prose) 2 x 30 minutes 15%
- **Unseen texts:** non-fiction texts (persuasive/informative) 1 hour 15%

WRITING EN3
- **Writing to advise, inform, explain or describe** 1 hour 15%
- **Writing to argue, persuade or instruct** 1 hour 15%

Examiner's Top Tip
Try answering questions against the clock – some questions only give you 30 minutes. You will find suggestions for exam practice in the exam sections of this book.

HOW TO BEGIN YOUR REVISION

✔ **KNOW YOUR COURSE REQUIREMENTS.** If you know what the requirements of the course are then you will stand a much better chance of meeting them. Make sure that you understand how your course is set out. Ask your teacher for advice and what you can expect to face in your exams. Look at past exam papers fairly early in your course, as these will help you understand what you have to aim for to get a good mark.

✔ **COMPLETE YOUR COURSE-WORK.** You <u>cannot</u> <u>get</u> <u>a</u> <u>good</u> <u>grade</u> unless <u>all</u> <u>your</u> <u>course-work</u> <u>is</u> <u>completed</u>. If you have worked steadily throughout the two-year course you should be fine. You can always submit new assignments to get better grades, providing that you are not overdoing it by racing to catch up with your course-work in several subjects. If you fall behind with your assignments you risk producing poor ones by rushing them.

Examiner's Top Tip
Revise all aspects of punctuation early in your course because this will help you to produce better course-work and it will also give you more confidence for your final exams.

✔ **PRODUCE A REVISION TIMETABLE.** Time management is crucial at every stage in your revision, not just in the exams themselves. You will relieve the pressure on yourself if you manage your time properly, allotting time to every part of the exam.
- Leave yourself time to relax and do not overdo it! If you try <u>too</u> hard you could end up doing your best work outside the exam room because you are <u>too</u> tired and stale.
- Go to bed in good time and do not be tempted to stay up late doing last-minute revision.
- Allow a few days in your revision timetable in which you do nothing at all. You will recharge your batteries and be the better for it. Again, if you do not understand something, have a short break and return to the problem later on. This works because your brain is still unconsciously puzzling things out while you are doing something else. When you start your revision again the problem may seem simple to solve.

✔ **STICK WITH IT.** A little and often is better for the mind than doing a lot, rarely. That is how people learn foreign languages.

✔ **BE CONFIDENT.** If you have done everything possible during your revision you should then be able to give a good account of yourself. Go into the exam hall with the idea of doing yourself justice! Show examiners what you know but remember to keep your points relevant. You will probably only use a fraction of what you know in the exam, which is why it is important to be selective in how you present your ideas.

✔ **BEGIN NOW.** Pair up with a friend if this helps to motivate you. You can divide up the work and report your findings to each other. Why not proof-read each other's work? You will get better at spotting your mistakes.

CATCHING UP ON MISSING ASSIGNMENTS OR PRODUCING BETTER ONES

It is easy to miss an assignment or leave it so late that another one gets in the way. Maybe you are dissatisfied with a course-work assignment that you rushed. Perhaps you thought that you could have done a better one.

In each of the course-work sections that follow at least one alternative catch-up assignment will be suggested. If you use an idea from this book for a catch-up assignment, remember to clear it with your teacher first. Your teacher is the one who has to submit your course-work to the exam board and do all the paperwork.

PUNCTUATION AGAIN!

- **Why? You may be still surviving on skills learned in Year 8.**
- **You cannot get good grades in English Language unless you can punctuate your writing skilfully and correctly.**

WHY USE PUNCTUATION?

- **When you speak,** you punctuate naturally through your pauses and body language. However, <u>when you write you have to help your reader understand what you mean through a variety of punctuation marks.</u> The more you know about punctuation the better you will be able to express yourself. Pupils who use <u>semi-colons and colons</u> stand out from others, especially if they use these punctuation marks effectively.

- **Writing** is a <u>second-hand way of getting our meaning across</u> to others; we need to punctuate our work to help our audience understand us. Remember that when we let our writing pass into the hands of others, our punctuation marks and the words we use to express ourselves are all that there is to communicate our message. We are no longer in a position to put right any errors, as we would be if we were speaking directly to our audience.

- **To sum up** we use punctuation marks to <u>clarify</u> the points and ideas that we want to communicate to others.

punctuation marks

INTERNET

Have a look at this for info on punctuation:
http://www.kidslangarts.about.com/kids/kidslangarts/cs/punctuation

Examiner's Top Tip
Markers can miss good points and ideas in your writing when their attention is continually drawn to punctuation errors.

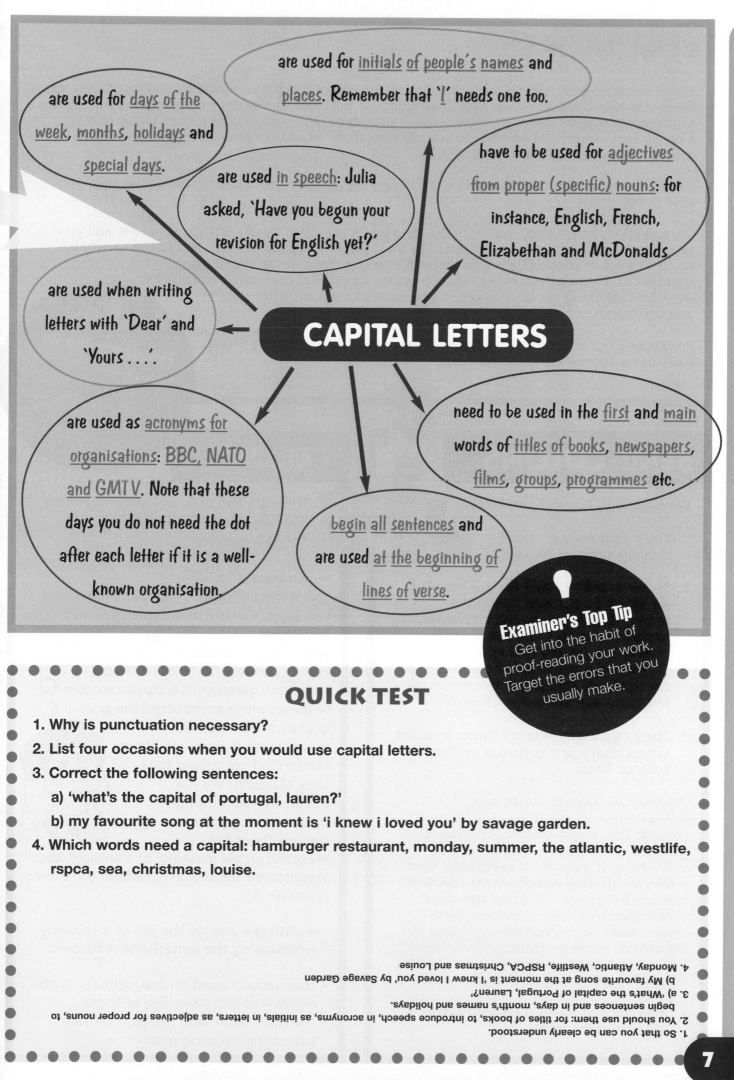

are used for <u>initials</u> <u>of</u> <u>people's</u> <u>names</u> and <u>places</u>. Remember that '<u>I</u>' needs one too.

are used for <u>days of the week</u>, <u>months</u>, <u>holidays</u> and <u>special days</u>.

are used <u>in speech</u>: Julia asked, 'Have you begun your revision for English yet?'

have to be used for <u>adjectives from proper (specific) nouns</u>: for instance, English, French, Elizabethan and McDonalds.

are used when writing letters with 'Dear' and 'Yours . . .'.

CAPITAL LETTERS

are used as <u>acronyms for organisations</u>: <u>BBC</u>, <u>NATO</u> and <u>GMTV</u>. Note that these days you do not need the dot after each letter if it is a well-known organisation.

need to be used in the <u>first</u> and <u>main</u> words of <u>titles of books</u>, <u>newspapers</u>, <u>films</u>, <u>groups</u>, <u>programmes</u> etc.

<u>begin</u> <u>all</u> <u>sentences</u> and are used <u>at the beginning of lines of verse</u>.

Examiner's Top Tip
Get into the habit of proof-reading your work. Target the errors that you usually make.

QUICK TEST

1. Why is punctuation necessary?
2. List four occasions when you would use capital letters.
3. Correct the following sentences:
   a) 'what's the capital of portugal, lauren?'
   b) my favourite song at the moment is 'i knew i loved you' by savage garden.
4. Which words need a capital: hamburger restaurant, monday, summer, the atlantic, westlife, rspca, sea, christmas, louise.

FULL STOPS

This is the main punctuation mark that signals the <u>end</u> of <u>one</u> <u>idea</u> <u>and</u> <u>the</u> <u>beginning</u> of <u>another</u>. Sentences help complete ideas in your writing. Use full stops to make <u>strong points</u> in your writing as they slow readers down. If you want your readers to mull over what you have to say or if you have an important point to make, use a full stop. If you want your readers to read your ideas quickly, use <u>semi-colons</u> or <u>colons</u>.

To get high grades in GCSE you will need to <u>vary</u> <u>the</u> <u>length</u> <u>of</u> <u>your</u> <u>sentences</u> and the <u>style</u> of your punctuation.

<u>Change</u> <u>your</u> <u>sentences</u> <u>by</u> <u>making</u> <u>some</u> <u>long</u> <u>and</u> <u>some</u> <u>short</u>; variety is the spice of life and your task is to keep your audience interested in what you want to say. You can add to the variety by using a range of <u>connective</u> words that will also give you a range of <u>expressive</u> possibilities. Try to be expressive through your choice of punctuation. If you want to describe something use <u>semi-colons</u>; if you want to make effective <u>statements</u> and <u>commands</u> use <u>full</u> <u>stops</u>.

Read your work aloud and listen to where one idea ends and another begins. Each idea is a sentence. Trust your ears.

SEMI-COLONS

<u>Semi-colons</u> <u>have</u> <u>many</u> <u>uses</u>.

- **They join two or more closely related ideas:**

1. **Steve worked hard for his results; he stuck to his revision plan.**
2. **Spring has come early; the trees have begun to blossom and the grassy banks are full of daffodils.**
3. **There are a number of good movies on tonight; just after the news on ITV they are showing Clueless.**

- **They separate sets of items in a list when there are commas within the sets or lists:**

When you unpack your new computer and set it up you should follow the loose-leaf instructions packed with your computer; you will then, if you look carefully, find everything you need: multi-coloured leads; the plugs for your monitor and base unit; the speakers with their leads; a microphone, if this is included, with a stand; manuals for your computer and, if you are lucky, lots of interesting software.

- **You do not need a capital letter after a semi-colon.**

COLONS

These are two dots, one above the other and they signify a new sentence. They are used to:

➻ introduce a list:
You should bring to your exam: a watch, two pens, a pencil and a ruler, tissues and hope!

➻ introduce quotations:
Hamlet ponders: 'To be or not to be. That is the question.' It is also acceptable to use a comma to introduce this brief quotation from Hamlet.

➻ punctuate dialogue in plays:
Macbeth: If we should fail?
Lady Macbeth: We fail!
But screw your courage
to the sticking place,
And we'll not fail.

➻ expand on the meaning of a previous idea:
Tracy scored the highest grade in the exam: it was an A*.

A dash can also do the job of a colon by emphasising the sentence that follows:

- Tom had achieved fantastic results in his exams – he got As in five of them.
- The girls' team won the cup – Phyllis scored the deciding goal.

OTHER PUNCTUATION

EXCLAMATION MARKS
These marks help express surprise, anger, fear, joy and most other emotions. For instance: Louise! It is good to see you!

QUESTION MARKS
These marks can be used for <u>rhetorical questions</u> where no direct reply is expected, only mental agreement: 'Who could defend a statement like that?'. <u>They</u> <u>can</u> also <u>be</u> <u>used</u> <u>for</u> <u>requests</u> <u>for</u> <u>information</u>: 'What time is it?' You do not need a question mark for an <u>indirect</u> <u>question</u>: 'Siobhan asked me for a pen.'

PUNCTUATION THAT MARKS THE END OF A SENTENCE

Punctuation helps you express yourself clearly so that you can get your ideas across to others.

QUICK TEST

1. Which are the quickest to get through when reading: full stops or semi-colons?
2. Explain one of the things that semi-colons can do.
3. What is a sentence?
4. Can a colon introduce a list of items?
5. Can colons be used to introduce a quotation?
6. Give one other purpose for a colon.

Examiner's Top Tip
Look at how professional writers use punctuation as you read their work. Pause over some passages and think about the effectiveness of the punctuation.

1. Semi-colons
2. Link two closely related phrases or separate sets of items in a list where there are commas within the sets.
3. It usually expresses a single idea
4. Yes
5. Yes
6. To write another phrase which expands upon the meaning of the first, or punctuate dialogue in plays.

9

SPEECH, QUOTATION AND TITLE MARKS AND COMMAS

Examiner's Top Tip
We use commas, naturally, when we speak but be careful not use them instead of full stops in sentences.

The skilful use of punctuation marks can improve your expression.

COMMAS

Commas have a variety of uses.

> They can be used to <u>separate</u> <u>lists</u>: I would like three hamburgers, a cheeseburger, a large serving of fries and a coffee.
>
> They are used to <u>clarify</u> <u>sentences</u> that could be misleading: After a period of calm, students returned after the fire alarm.
>
> They need to be used in <u>direct</u> <u>speech</u>: Elaine was curious about the previous evening and asked, 'Where did you get to?'
> 'The shopping centre,' John replied.
>
> They can be used to mark off <u>words</u>, <u>phrases</u>, and <u>connectives</u> in sentences: Billy, who did not like to be made fun of, was angry. On the other hand, there was no harm in what Carly said.

Examiner's Top Tip
Whether you use double inverted commas or single ones in your direct speech – be consistent.

SPEECH

There are four main rules for setting out speech:

1. Use <u>inverted</u> <u>commas</u> for the words spoken: Catherine said, 'I haven't seen you in ages!'
2. <u>Direct</u> <u>speech</u> must be separated from the rest of the writing by a punctuation mark. See the comma in the example above.
3. Remember to use a <u>capital letter</u> when you begin the direct speech. The example with Catherine said, 'It's ages since I last saw you.'
4. Each time you introduce a <u>new speaker</u> begin a <u>new line</u> and <u>indent</u>. That is, begin the speech of your new speaker three letter spaces to the right of the margin.

QUOTATION MARKS

• These are inverted commas for words or phrases cited from texts. Stick with single inverted commas for speech and double inverted commas for speech within speech. For instance: Jane shouted to her husband in the next room, 'Your mother phoned and she said, "When are you going to visit me?" Colin, I thought that you called in on her last week.'

• <u>Remember</u> <u>to</u> <u>close</u> <u>them</u>. It is confusing for readers and markers if you fail to do so! To show that you are ending a quotation, place the final full stop on the outside of the inverted comma as with the following example. In My Fair Lady Eliza Doolittle shows her independence from Professor Higgins when she says, 'I can do without you.'

TITLE MARKS

• In secondary schools inverted commas are used to signify: book titles, stories, newspapers, magazines, television programmes, movies or shows. For example, 'My Fair Lady' is the title of the musical or 1964 film version of the play, 'Pygmalion'.

• In your writing always use title marks to show the difference between eponymous characters and the names of the plays and novels in which they appear: Macbeth is a character whereas 'Macbeth' is a play. (Eponymous characters share their name with the titles of their texts.)

• The convention (or accepted rule) for titles in universities is to underline them: <u>Hamlet</u> and **Macbeth**. The main thing is to remain consistent in your method of identifying titles.

• Note that if you use italics for titles then this is acceptable for printed work. Notice that in much of this book italics have been used for the titles of texts and films.

APOSTROPHES OF POSSESSION AND CONTRACTION

They help shorten words or show that something belongs to someone.

Key Fact

<u>Its and it's can be confusing words</u>. If you wrote, I emptied a box of its contents', you would not need an apostrophe. This is because 'its' in this instance is a possessive pronoun. On the other hand if you say, 'It's going to rain all day', you need an apostrophe because you mean 'it is'.

APOSTROPHES THAT SHOW POSSESSION

POSSESSIVE PRONOUNS
<u>Pronouns like these do not need apostrophes to show ownership</u>:
• my
• his
• hers
• yours
• its
• ours
• theirs

EXAMPLES
The computer is hers.
The watch is mine.
The house is theirs.
The bag is yours.

APOSTROPHES OF OWNERSHIP FOR ONE PERSON OR THING
If there is a <u>single</u> owner, place the apostrophe <u>before</u> the 's':
• Tim's video player
• Christine's house
• The sun's rays

APOSTROPHES OF OWNERSHIP FOR MORE THAN ONE OWNER
If there is <u>more than one</u> owner, you need to put the apostrophe <u>after</u> the 's' to show that you mean a <u>plural</u> owner:
• The Jacksons' video
• The Smiths' house

<u>If a person's name naturally ends in 's' you can do one of two things</u>:
• James's haircut
or
• James' haircut
• The Jones's house
Whichever style you go for, stick with it because readers and markers like you to remain consistent.

If a plural noun does <u>not</u> need an 's' to make it plural you should place your apostrophe <u>before</u> the 's':
• The men's business venture
• The women's society
• The children's playground
• The people's champion

EXPRESSION
You can vary your expression by using an apostrophe:
• 'The claws of the cat' becomes 'The cat's claws' with an apostrophe.
If you are unsure of where to put a possessive apostrophe then write your sentence the long way round:
• 'Dan's new house' becomes 'The new house of Dan'.
Always ask yourself why you are inserting an apostrophe. Do not put it in just for good measure.

APOSTROPHES THAT SHORTEN WORDS

- <u>Contractions</u> combine <u>two</u> words into <u>one</u> with an apostrophe.
- <u>Abbreviations</u> are words in which letters have been <u>missed</u> <u>out</u>. <u>Apostrophes</u> <u>are</u> <u>used</u> <u>to</u> <u>show</u> <u>that</u> <u>one</u> <u>or</u> <u>more</u> <u>letters</u> <u>have</u> <u>been</u> <u>missed</u> <u>out</u>.

I'm = I am   Won't = Will not

Doesn't = Does not   They're = They are

Can't = Cannot   Would've = Would have

Examiner's Top Tip
Apostrophes are marks that help readers understand the intention of the writer. Use them to convey meaning as fully as you can.

USE AN APOSTROPHE WHEN WRITING THE TIME
- 'I will see Dave at 7 o'clock.' This is the short way of writing 'seven of the clock'.
- Missing numbers in dates can be suggested by an apostrophe:
21st of September '99
3rd of November '01

APOSTROPHES IN PLAYS
Playwrights such as Shakespeare shortened their words to allow their verse to remain in <u>iambic</u> <u>pentameter</u>. Shakespeare tried to divide his blank-verse lines into <u>10 syllables</u>, that is, <u>five</u> <u>feet</u> of <u>two</u> <u>syllables</u> <u>each</u>. Take this example from Romeo and Juliet, in which Romeo wants to Juliet to exchange vows:
- Romeo: 'Th' exchange of thy love's faithful vow for mine.

APOSTROPHES IN DIALECT
Apostrophes are used a great deal by writers when they try to represent <u>local</u> <u>dialect</u>:
' 'ow's it goin' me ole mate?'
' 'awight, 'ow's it goin' yurself? I aint seen yu' in ages!'

QUICK TEST

True or false:

1. Possessive pronouns can take apostrophes.

2. Apostrophes lengthen words.

3. Apostrophes can help show ownership.

4. If a person's name ends with an 's' you can put the apostrophe after it.

5. I ca'nt is correct.

6. Apostrophes of possession can help vary your sentences and can make them shorter.

1. False
2. False
3. True
4. True
5. False
6. True

THE MAIN TYPES OF SENTENCES

THERE ARE FOUR MAIN TYPES OF SENTENCE:

1. STATEMENTS

Statements are the most common type of sentences and they usually give information:
- I will pair up with Joanne to start my revision on Tuesday.
- John called last night but you were out.
- My name is Heather.
- James wants to revise with us too.
- I found a five pound note fluttering in the street.

2. EXCLAMATIONS

Exclamations help writers express emotions in writing:
- How dare you!
- How could you say that!
- Oh God!
- Watch out!
- What a surprise!

3. INSTRUCTIONS OR COMMANDS

Instructions or commands tell you to do something; they are often used on notices:
- Don't look out of the window.
- Purchase a ticket before you travel.
- Only one seat per person.
- Insert your card this way up.
- Look both ways before you cross the road.
- We require telephone booking.

4. QUESTIONS

Questions are mostly requests for information:
- Have you started your revision yet?
- Will you come to the show?
- How are you?
- Can I have two tickets please?
- Do you have the time?

PARTS OF SPEECH FOUND IN SENTENCES

NOUNS

Nouns can be:
- PEOPLE: Martin, Steve, Celia-Jane, Deborah
- PLACES: Big Ben, Westminster, Covent Garden, shopping centre
- THINGS: mobile phones, computers, drinks
- IDEAS AND FEELINGS: love, hate, life, danger

ADJECTIVES

Adjectives describe nouns. They say what nouns look, seem or feel like.

Examples:
- *black coffee*
- *blue Monday*
- *great movie*
- *dark wood*
- *wild weekend*

VERBS

Verbs are 'doing' or action words.
Examples
- *'swim', 'talk', 'walk', 'be'*
- *Tim revises every second day (revises).*
- *Jane works hard at her studies (works).*

ADVERBS

Adverbs say more about verbs. They explain how, when and where something is happening.
Example:
After the movie had ended the girls stood outside the cinema. Heather and Adriane listened carefully to Francesca because she always talked incredibly quickly and enthusiastically when she was excited by a movie. She always said amazingly clever things about them too. Afterwards, the friends agreed to meet inside the cinema foyer to see another movie early in the evening the next day. They hoped to buy their tickets before any queues began to form.
- *Notice how many adverbs end in 'ly'. These –ly adverbs explain how, while other adverbs say more about the time and place as they qualify the nouns to which they refer.*

PREPOSITIONS

Prepositions join up words and keep them in order.
Examples:
- *Lucy looked behind the mirror and under the dressing table.*
- *John was beside the lake when his friends pushed him in.*
- *Louise put her mobile in her bag to take it on her shopping trip with her.*
- *When Phil looked for his passport he could not find it – he left it behind on the kitchen table!*
- *John asked Laura, a lively girl with ginger hair, if she would go with him to the show.*

Prepositions include:
- *for, in, on, from, at, over, under, beside, within, before, around, above, to, and many more.*

HOW SENTENCES ARE FORMED

WORDS CAN BE GROUPED IN THREE DIFFERENT WAYS:

Phrases
Phrases are groups of words (two or more) or sayings without a verb:
- fish and chips
- dashing and dynamic
- chatty and cheerful
- beans on toast
- dangerously handsome
- black and white

Clauses
Clauses are groups of words that have a verb:
- he said goodbye
- she bought a magazine
- Adriane swam the length of the pool

Sentences
Sentences are groups of words that have at least one clause. They usually have: a full stop, colon, semi-colon, question mark or an exclamation mark to conclude them.

INDEPENDENT AND DEPENDENT CLAUSES
Independent or main clauses can stand on their own as sentences.
Dependent or subclauses often begin with words like 'since' or 'if'.

- I bought a fish supper because I like fish and chips. (independent)
  because I like fish and chips (dependent).
- When she arrives at school Denise is dashing and dynamic. (independent)
  when she arrives at school (dependent)
- The pupils are chatty and cheerful because they passed their exams. (independent)
  because they passed their exams (dependent)
- James ate beans on toast because he was very hungry. (independent)
  because he was very hungry (dependent)
- Since his new haircut Philip is dangerously handsome. (independent)
  since his new haircut (dependent)
- Not all arguments are black and white when you look into them. (independent)
- when you look into them. (dependent)

Notice how:
- independent clauses make sense on their own as sentences.
- dependent clauses cannot stand on their own in sentences. They need an independent clause joined onto them before they can make a sentence.
- an independent clause can be placed at the beginning or the end of the dependent clause.

SENTENCES

QUICK TEST

True or false:

1. A phrase can be a sentence.

2. Independent clauses can make sense on their own.

3. 'When you look into them' is a sentence.

4. The sentence, 'Write your name in block capitals' is a statement.

5. Varying your sentences can improve your expression.

6. 'Blue' in 'blue moon' is a verb.

7. 'Inside' is a preposition.

8. 'Carefully' in 'Sabrina carefully picks up the glass' is an adverb.

9. The name Geraldine is a noun.

10. 'Freedom' is a verb.

10. False
9. True
8. True
7. True
6. False
5. True
4. False. It is a command or an instruction.
3. False
2. True
1. False

SPELLINGS AND WAYS TO LEARN THEM

METHODS OF LEARNING TRICKY SPELLINGS

1. The first piece of advice seems obvious, yet it is surprising how little it is taken – <u>look up words in dictionaries and check their spellings</u>. Dictionaries work on the alphabet principle for each word and finding words becomes easier with practice. <u>Carry a small dictionary with you</u>. Relying on teachers and others to spell words for you means that you will never really learn them. <u>Aim to be an independent learner</u>.

2. <u>The Look–Cover–Say–Write–Check</u> method is a successful one as long as you have spelled the word correctly in the first place. Learning words by repeating this process does work.

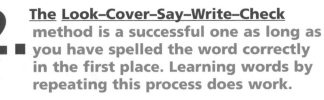

3. Try writing <u>**a crazy but memorable sentence**</u> using each letter of the word <u>**(a mnemonic)**</u>. Take for example, the word <u>**believe**</u>. **B**ig **e**lephants **l**ook **i**nside **e**lephantine **v**ases **e**very-where. Only use this method for the few words that are the biggest bugbears for you, otherwise you will have too many strange phrases to remember.

4. <u>Use the sound of words to help you spell them</u>. Work your way through each syllable as you aim to spell the word. This works for many words and is always worth trying before using other methods.

5. For <u>**tricky plural endings**</u> follow these rules: If a noun ends with a '<u>**y**</u>' and it has a consonant such as 'a', 't', 'r' or 'n' before the y, you need to add '<u>**ies**</u>' to the plural. **EXAMPLE** dia<u>r</u>y – diaries, cur<u>r</u>y – curries, compa<u>n</u>y – companies, ci<u>t</u>y – cities

6. If the **last letter before the '<u>y</u>'** is a vowel (a, e, i, o, u) you have to add an '<u>**s**</u>' to make the plural. **EXAMPLE** b<u>o</u>y – boys, journ<u>e</u>y – journeys, k<u>e</u>y – keys, g<u>u</u>y – guys, monkey –monkeys

7. Words which end in '<u>**fe**</u>' such as knife take '<u>**ves**</u>' in plurals; similarly words ending in '<u>**f**</u>' like <u>**shelf**</u> or <u>**half**</u> change to <u>**shelves**</u> and <u>**halves**</u> in plurals.

8. <u>Use 'i' before 'e' except after 'c'</u>. For example, <u>**receive**</u>.

<u>Proof-read</u> your work for words that you know you are likely to get wrong. <u>Make a list of these words from a number of subjects and focus on learning them</u>.

BRITISH AND AMERICAN SPELLINGS

You need to be aware of the variation between British and American spellings. The Americans tend to drop unnecessary letters in their words.

BRITISH	AMERICAN
cancelled	canceled
centre	center
cheque	check
colour	color
criticise	criticize
grey	gray
humour	humor
honour	honor
jewellery	jewelry
judgement	judgment
labour	labor
licence	license
organisation	organization
okay	o.k.
programme	program
realise	realize
theatre	theater
tyre	tire
valour	valor

Examiner's Top Tip
If you cannot think of the correct spelling of a word in an exam, try to use a similar word that you can spell.

Points to Remember

- Be careful to use British and not American spellings.
- We use an 's' in words where the Americans use a 'z'.
- Use 'i' before 'e' except after 'c'.
- Proof-read your work for the errors that you know you are likely to make.

QUICK TEST

Examiner's Top Tip
Accurate spelling is important. Misspelled work distracts your readers and examiners from fully appreciating your ideas.

Circle the correct spelling:

1. a) intrested b) interested c) interrested
2. a) difinitely b) definately c) definitely
3. a) disappear b) dissapear c) dissappear
4. a) neccessary b) necessary c) necessary
5. a) embarrass b) embarass c) embarras
6. a) seperate b) saperete c) separate
7. a) recieve b) receive c) receave

1. b
2. c
3. a
4. b
5. a
6. c
7. b

A CHECKLIST OF WORDS OFTEN MISSPELLED

EASILY MISSPELLED WORDS

A–F
accelerator
acquire
a lot (use two words)
angel
answer
appearance
arguing
argument
audience
banned
before
beginning
behaviour
believable
believe
beware
calm
careful
cemetery
character
clause
climbed
comma
compare
complete
completely
compromise
conjunction
cupboard
dangerous
decide
definitely
devastating
dialect
dialled
different
disappear
disappointment
discuss
disguise
doesn't

don't
effectively
elderly
embarrass
examination
excellent
excited
extremely
families
family
fault
finally
foreign
fought
future

G–P
goodbye
grammar
guess
guilty
hear
here (place)
hypocrisy
imagine
independence
individual
intelligence
intelligent
interested
interview
intriguing
issues
its meaning
it's (it is)
jealous
jewellery
kept
knife
knives
laid (past tense as in the hens laid eggs)

leisure
lie (to tell a lie)
lie or lay (on a bed)
lounge
lying
meant
Mediterranean
metaphor
minutes
necessary
necessity
only
partner
peculiar
people
piece
planned
polite
possess
practice (noun)
practise (verb)
preferred
principal (college head)
principle (point of honour)
privilege
probably
proceed
professional
putting

R–W
racism
receive
reckon
recommend
rehearse
relationship
relevant
relieved
reply

restaurant
rhythm
sense
sentence
separate
seriously
sincere
sincerely
skilful
snapped
special
squashed
squeaky
stopped
stories
story
straight
succeed
surprise
thought
threw (verb)
through (adverb)
tired
toilet
tongue
tragedy
truly
trustworthy
twelfth
unnecessary
until/till
vehicle
weird
wilful

HOMOPHONES

These are words that are easily confused because they sound the same.

CHECKLIST OF WORDS OFTEN MISSPELLED

Examiner's Top Tip
Always proof-read your work. Identify the spellings that you have most trouble with and check these ones first.

accept	**agree to**	**led**	**to lead**
except	exclude	lead	metal
affect	**verb**	**peace**	**quiet**
effect	noun	piece	bit
allowed	**let**	**practise**	**verb**
aloud	loudly	practice	noun
bored	**fed up**	**principal**	college head
board	game	principle	point of honour
break	**shatter**	**quiet**	silence
brake	slow down	quite	adverb
buy	**purchase**	**right**	**correct/direction**
bye	goodbye	write	with a pen
college	**education**	**there**	**place**
collage	painting	their	ownership
queue	**line of people**	**they're**	**they are**
cue	for actors/snooker	threw	verb
dept.	**department**	through	adverb
debt	to owe	**to**	**preposition**
fair	**just**	two	number
fare	ticket	too	also/very
hear	**sounds**	**were**	**plural of 'was'**
here	place	where	question
knew	**to know**	whether	or not
new	unused	weather	sun and rain

SYNONYMS

Examiner's Top Tip
English is a notoriously difficult language to spell but with effort you can overcome most obvious misspellings. There are people who can spell well and those who do not make serious effort! Why not go through the lists here and try some of the exercises suggested on the previous pages? The main one is: Look–Cover–Say–Write–Check.

These are words that mean the same.

EXAMPLES

beautiful = pretty, nice, fine, good-looking, elegant, lovely, fair.

display = show, exhibit, exhibition, spread, open, expose, demonstration. layout.

19

PUTTING YOUR IDEAS IN THE RIGHT ORDER

WORDS THAT HELP PUT YOUR IDEAS IN ORDER
· firstly, then, so far, secondly, in the end, next, eventually, subsequently, at last, at length, afterwards

WORDS FOR EXCEPTIONS
· only, if, unless, except (for), save for

Examiner's Top Tip
The skilful use of connectives can help you vary your sentence structure and improve your style.

MAKING POINTS AND GIVING EXAMPLES

WORDS TO USE TO ARGUE AND MAKE POINTS
• consequently, thus, so, as a result, because, as, hence, therefore, since, until, whenever, accordingly, as long as

WORDS TO HELP YOU GIVE EXAMPLES
• for example, for instance, such as, take the case of, thus, as (evidence), to show that, as revealed by

WORDS FOR EXTRA POINTS OR IDEAS
• and, too, what is more, also, furthermore, and then, again, moreover, as well as, in addition

WORDS WHICH HELP YOU EMPHASISE POINTS
• above all, in particular, notably, specifically, indeed, more important, especially, significant(ly), in fact

PARAGRAPHING

Paragraphs are necessary to give the readers a rest and help them to follow the writer's meaning.
• Paragraphs are groups of sentences connected by the same topic. Each paragraph carries a main idea.
• The main sentence of a paragraph is often found at the beginning and it is called a topic sentence. For example: Successful students plan their revision in each subject. They plan how much time they have available and then try to cover a number of areas in each subject.
• Any paragraphs following the first paragraph will need to begin on a new line, indented 2 cm from the page margin. In business correspondence or word-processed work there is no need to indent new paragraphs.
• You can link your paragraphs together skilfully by using the connecting words found in boxes on these pages.

BEING PERSUASIVE AND ANALYTICAL

WORDS TO PERSUADE
• of course, naturally, obviously, clearly, certainly, surely, evidently

WORDS TO HELP YOU SHOW AN OPINION OR ANALYSE
• it would seem, to suggest, one might conclude/propose/deduce/infer/imply/say/consider

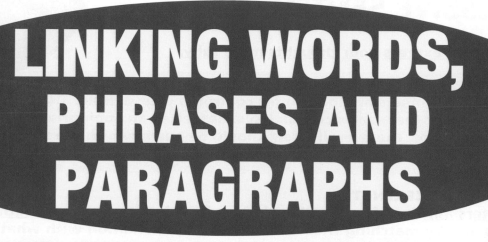

LINKING WORDS, PHRASES AND PARAGRAPHS

COMPARING AND CONTRASTING

WORDS TO MAKE A CONTRAST OR SHOW WHAT IS DIFFERENT
• *but, nevertheless, alternatively, despite this, on the contrary, however, yet, the opposite, instead, whereas, to turn to, although, still, on the other hand*

WORDS TO COMPARE THINGS IN YOUR WRITING – WHAT IS THE SAME?
• *equally, in the same way, as with, likewise, similarly, compared with, an equivalent*

ESSAY ENDINGS

WORDS TO SUM UP OR END WITH
• in brief, in summary, throughout, in all, on the whole, to sum up, overall, finally, to conclude, to recap, in the end

QUICK TEST

1. Why use paragraphs?
2. Identify two words that can help you compare pieces of writing.
3. What is the difference between comparing and contrasting?
4. Give two words that help emphasise points in writing.
5. What do these words help you to do: 'further more' and 'moreover'.

1. Paragraphs help readers follow your ideas. They also break up too much text which readers can find off-putting.
2. In the same way, similarly, equally, as with, likewise, compared with, an equivalent.
3. To 'compare' is to look for similarities and to 'contrast' is to look for differences
4. Indeed, in particular, above all, notably, specifically, more importantly, especially, significantly(ly), in fact (any of these).
5. They help you make extra points or ideas

IMPROVE YOUR STYLE AND MAKE YOUR WRITING MORE EXPRESSIVE

Examiner's Top Tip
Try to improve your expression as you develop the habit of proof-reading your work. The Russian writer Chekhov said, 'Rewrite everything five times!'

EXPRESSIVE SENTENCES

These help you express your thoughts more fully.

CONTROL

Teachers and examiners are looking for **control** in your writing. That is, an aware-ness of the effect that sentences can have, as well as an appropriate choice of words within them. The overall effect should be one in which the writer's meaning is expressed through **well-chosen words** placed in **skilfully constructed sentences**.

VARYING SENTENCE LENGTH

Good writers aim for effects within their writing by varying the length of their sentences and by matching their sentences and punctuation with what they are writing about.

HOW TO BUILD TENSION

You can build a tense atmosphere by keeping your sentences short. For example, in a **horror story** you can show **fear** and **tension** through using **short, darting** sentences. In this passage the first-person narrator endures a chase through a wood on a dark night:

'I ran. Ran for all I was worth! Sometimes I stumbled over tree roots. Branches slashed my face. Something was rapidly hunting me down. Twigs and branches snapped in the desperate rushing behind me. A savage, wolf-like howl tore the air. Something clasped my leg! "God help me!" I screamed, as I gasped for breath.'

THE EFFECT OF REVERSING WORDS AND PHRASES

Notice how writing can be more expressive when you **reverse** the expected order of a sentence. Rather than 'I stumbled over tree roots sometimes,' the randomness of the stumbling is enhanced by putting 'sometimes I stumbled' at the beginning of the sentence. Play around with what goes where in your sentences. It is by such tinkering that **expression**, and eventually your own **style**, will develop.

DESCRIPTION

Descriptive writing should involve **longer, more detailed sentences with adjectives saying more about nouns and adverbs modifying verbs**. Such writing may have semi-colons because readers would be expected to read this type of writing quite quickly.

OVERDOING DESCRIPTION

However, take care not to **over-decorate** your prose (writing) because you will want your audience to understand what you mean and not get sidetracked by too much description. Use **metaphors, personification** and **similes** sparingly. Used in this manner such **figurative language** will set off your writing effectively by making your points more striking as well as keeping your meaning clear.

UNNECESSARY REPETITION

Avoid using tautologies; that is repeating yourself unnecessarily. Also try to avoid reinforcing words with words that would be better left out. Your writing will have more impact without them. Tautologies to avoid:

- final end
- sad misfortune
- puzzling mystery

Word-reinforcement to avoid
- totally wrong
- absolutely fantastic
- seriously consider

CLARITY AND BREVITY

Keep what you write brief, simple and clear. Avoid long-winded, pompous sentences.
- 'I remained in my abode and passed the time watching uninteresting programmes while looking at the little box in the corner.'

This is tedious. Try this instead:
- 'I stayed at home watching boring programmes on TV.'

OVERWORKED INFORMAL WORDS

Avoid overworked words because they can be boring and repetitive.

Examples:
- got, get, nice, good, totally, a lot of, kind of

These are too casual to be used as formal, standard English.

CIRCUMLOCUTIONS

Circumlocutions are roundabout ways of saying things. Again, stick to simple words or expressions, as these are more effective.
- few in number = few
- in a majority of cases = usually
- in less than no time = quickly
- in the event that = if
- on the grounds that = because
- owing to the fact that = because
- prior to = before
- with the exception of = except

HOW TO IMPROVE YOUR EXPRESSION

CLICHÉS

Clichés are tired expressions and imagery that have lost any impact because of overuse. There are, of course, a host of such worn-out phrases often reached for by tired minds. Avoid the following:
- like the plague
- like two ships that pass in the night
- food for thought
- leaves much to be desired
- leave no stone unturned
- shoot oneself in the foot
- we will deliver (that is, doing something – a favourite cliché of politicians!)

WRITING EFFECTIVE SENTENCES

For a stylish, effective sentence the importance of each part is as follows:
- the beginning is the second-most important part
- the middle is least important
- the end is the most important.

Take, for example, this line from Shakespeare's *Twelfth Night* given to Malvolio: 'Some are born great, some achieve greatness and some have greatness thrust upon 'em.'

QUICK TEST

1. Reduce these phrases to one word:

a) Due to the fact that

b) Pink in colour

c) In this day and age

2. What is the danger of overdoing description?

3. Identify a cliché and explain why you should try to avoid clichés in writing.

3. 'Shot in the foot'. The image has no impact and will simply pass readers by, or worse, bore them. There are numerous examples.
2. The readers could lose sight of your meaning.
1. a) because b) pink c) now

SPEAKING AND LISTENING

HOW YOU WILL BE GRADED

- Can you speak with purpose in a structured way? You need to signpost your points when you speak so that others can follow what you are saying and do not get bored.

- Are you able to speak with fluency and confidence on your chosen topic with minimal notes? Do not make the mistake of reading your notes. Someone with their head stuck in their notes, losing their place and starting their points again is not very impressive.

- Do you vary the sound of your voice to interest your audience? Do you use eye contact and other body language to interest your listener? Sixty per cent of any communication is non-verbal! This means that you use body language such as posture, hand gestures and eye contact as well as varying the tone and pitch of your voice when you speak. This is how people understand what you mean. All these things are converted into punctuation when you write down what you are saying. Writing is therefore a very poor substitute for speaking. It is difficult to get exactly what you mean across to someone when you write because you are not usually there to animate your words.

- Can you adapt the register of your speech to the task and your audience? You would hardly speak to your head-teacher using the same tone of voice as you would to your best friends. You need to be conscious of how people adapt their speech to those they talk to.

- Are you able to use standard English with confidence in a range of situations? How fluent is your standard English? Do you drop into your local dialect without realising that you are doing so? You need to be more conscious of when you use dialect as well as why, where and to whom you would use standard English. If you were answering a phone in an office you would not use local dialect. It all comes down to being polite, especially with people we do not know. They need to understand us.

- Can you initiate speech, sustain a point of view or manage the contributions of others? If so, you would make a great host of a discussion panel.

- Can you listen with sensitivity and respond accordingly? Are you able to carry forward and further the arguments of others and follow a complex conversation?

CAN YOU:
- skilfully involve listeners?
- speak with irony?
- show flair or make thought-provoking contributions?
- show that you have a wide vocabulary?
- use rhetorical techniques?

Examiner's Top Tip
Take turns in speaking and show that you listen!

WHAT YOU WILL DO

<u>You will need to do a minimum of three orals</u>, at least one of each of the following:

SINGLE ORAL
Pick a subject that only you could talk about. Choose something that you know really well and would enjoy talking about.

PAIRED ORAL
This is a good one in which to analyse junk mail, a poem or any story. Maybe you would like to look at an issue in the news and explore and analyse it?

GROUP
<u>Excellent for debates and anything to do with teamwork.</u>

- <u>You can do more than three orals but only your best grades in each set of criteria will be counted;</u> so do as many as you can! The orals can be done in any order so long as you have covered the objectives on the right.
- <u>It is advisable to keep a written record of your oral.</u> If you do, then you need to give some details of what the oral was about. Then explain how the oral went.
- You should say what went well and identify areas for <u>improvement</u>.
- Some activities will also cover more than one set of criteria so it is therefore acceptable (sometimes) to cover the same criteria twice.

These are the three main marking criteria for the orals that you have to do:

EXPLAIN, DESCRIBE OR NARRATE
This is good for autobiographical stories, work placements, explaining a story that you have written, your main hobby, etc.

EXPLORE, ANALYSE OR IMAGINE
This can be very wide-ranging. Good things to talk about here are persuasive techniques in junk mail and the imagery and themes of poems, stories, etc.

DISCUSS, ARGUE OR PERSUADE
Great for debates, burning issues that concern your life, topics in the news, etc. Maybe something could be debated out of a poem, story or novel that you have read in class. For instance, is Tess of the D'Urbervilles really 'A Pure Woman' as the subtitle of the book suggests?

Examiner's Top Tip
Try to relax when you do your orals. Remember that this is a chance to boost your grades. Your teacher knows you and will want to give you the highest grade that you deserve.

STANDARD ENGLISH

· <u>This is formal, the English you should use with people that you do not know.</u> The aim is to be clearly understood by anyone. Teachers usually use it! In other words, do not use 'Me and Danielle ain't saw each other for ages' when 'Danielle and I have not seen each other for ages' is called for.
· In formal situations avoid your <u>local dialect</u>. This should be used for talking to your family, friends or neighbours. <u>There is nothing wrong with dialect. It is the correct, friendly language to use in informal situations</u>. Use it when you talk to your friends and family. It is alright then to say, "'ere, mate, could ya pass us the bu''er.'

QUICK TEST

1. How many orals do you need to take and what must each of them be?
2. What is standard English and when should you use it?
3. Why would you use body language?
4. With whom would you use dialect?
5. Why is it important to listen?

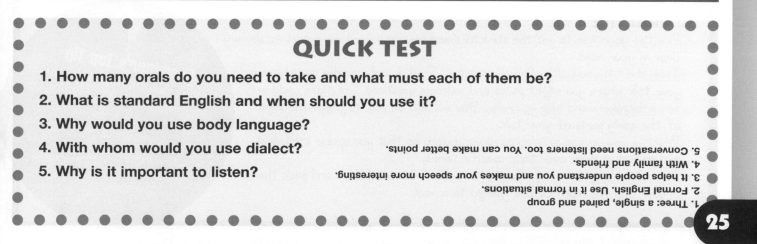

5. Conversations need listeners too. You can make better points.
4. With family and friends.
3. It helps people understand you and makes your speech more interesting.
2. Formal English. Use it in formal situations.
1. Three: a single, paired and group

SPEAKING AND LISTENING: PREPARING AND GIVING A TALK

By choosing/buying this book you have shown that <u>you</u> <u>have</u> <u>initiative</u> and that <u>you</u> <u>are</u> <u>an</u> <u>independent</u> <u>learner</u>. Why not try this:
- *With a partner, talk about how a leaflet <u>informs</u>, <u>explains</u> or <u>describes</u>.*
- *Show how some leaflets <u>persuade</u>, <u>discuss</u> and <u>argue</u>.*
- *Save and use any interesting <u>junk</u> <u>mail</u> that arrives through your letterbox. In particular, look for letters written by charities and anything with interesting fonts and pictures. Other good sources for excellent leaflets are public libraries, and doctors' and dentists' surgeries.*
- *<u>See</u> <u>the</u> <u>checklist</u> <u>in</u> 'Language and Layout' <u>of</u> <u>the</u> <u>media</u> <u>section</u> <u>of</u> <u>this</u> <u>book</u> <u>on</u> <u>pages</u> <u>40–41</u> <u>to</u> <u>help</u> <u>you</u> <u>prepare</u> <u>for</u> <u>this</u> <u>talk.</u>*

PREPARING YOUR TALK

1. THE TOPIC
- <u>If</u> <u>you</u> <u>are</u> <u>allowed,</u> <u>choose</u> <u>a</u> <u>topic</u> <u>that</u> <u>interests</u> <u>you</u>. It could be your work placement or perhaps a hobby or a mania.
- Your talk will be to:

  - explain, describe or narrate - explore, analyse or imagine - discuss, argue or persuade

- <u>Think of a suitable title for your talk.</u> This will help you <u>focus</u> on your topic.
- <u>Research</u> your topic. Talk to experts; do some research on the Internet; look in encyclopedias; check out your library; write to agencies, companies or embassies.
- <u>Gather resources to help you with your details,</u> points and arguments. Find and prepare any <u>props</u> that you need now. They will be useful for focusing and keeping your audience's attention on what you are saying.

2. THE STRUCTURE
- <u>Think</u> <u>about</u> <u>the structure of your talk: introduction, body and conclusion.</u>
- <u>Summarise</u> the talk in a few paragraphs. Keep them brief.
- <u>Brainstorm</u> your talk into a flow chart.

3. THE PROMPTS
- Cut up several square pieces of card just smaller than a postcard.
- Write down your <u>main ideas</u> in words or phrases to remind you of what you intend to say. <u>Resist the temptation to write too much.</u> Keep to brief points because you will use them as prompts.
- <u>Write the words or phrases twice the size of your normal writing.</u> This is for your own self-assurance as you speak. If you forget your next point just glance at your card. Turn over the cards as you speak.
- <u>Spread out your cards on a table and pick them up in the correct order.</u> Number the cards in the right order. The structure of your talk will then be clear for you as well as your audience.

4. PRACTICE
- <u>Practise your talk</u> to get the structure and any <u>specialised</u> or <u>unusual vocabulary</u> clear in your mind.
- <u>Think about the necessity of using standard English</u> and consider any places in your talk where you might pause and welcome questions. <u>Questions could act as ice-breakers and help you relax.</u> You will also be able to gauge the impact of the early parts of your talk.
- <u>Practise any unusual or specialised vocabulary</u> so that you appear confident and do not stumble over topic-specific terms.
- <u>Remember to get props or handouts ready</u> if you need them and pack them in your bag the night before you go to school.

Examiner's Top Tip
Remember to show that you are also a good listener. Do not talk over people. Take turns in speech. However, you do need to say something in group talks, otherwise it will be impossible for your teacher to assess you fully.

GIVING THE TALK

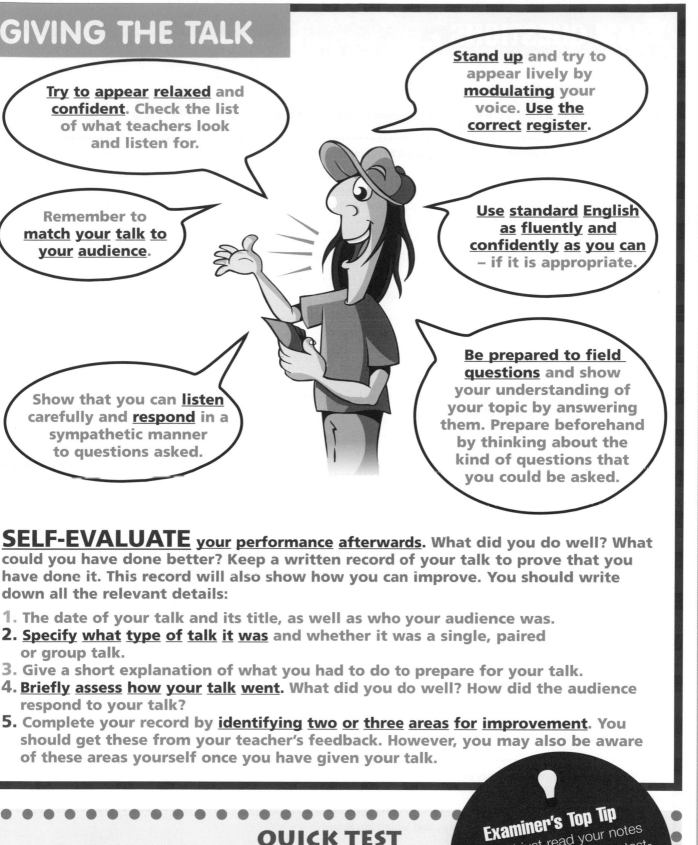

Try to appear relaxed and **confident**. Check the list of what teachers look and listen for.

Stand up and try to appear lively by **modulating** your voice. **Use the correct register**.

Remember to match your talk to your audience.

Use standard English as fluently and confidently as you can – if it is appropriate.

Show that you can **listen** carefully and **respond** in a sympathetic manner to questions asked.

Be prepared to field questions and show your understanding of your topic by answering them. Prepare beforehand by thinking about the kind of questions that you could be asked.

SELF-EVALUATE your performance afterwards. What did you do well? What could you have done better? Keep a written record of your talk to prove that you have done it. This record will also show how you can improve. You should write down all the relevant details:

1. The date of your talk and its title, as well as who your audience was.
2. **Specify what type of talk it was** and whether it was a single, paired or group talk.
3. Give a short explanation of what you had to do to prepare for your talk.
4. **Briefly assess how your talk went**. What did you do well? How did the audience respond to your talk?
5. Complete your record by **identifying two or three areas for improvement**. You should get these from your teacher's feedback. However, you may also be aware of these areas yourself once you have given your talk.

QUICK TEST

1. Why is it important to plan your talk?
2. Towards the end of your talk what might you do to involve your audience?
3. What is standard English?

3. This is formal English in which you pronounce all your words correctly and avoid using local dialect.
2. Ask questions or show them props.
1. It helps give a more coherent structure and more detail.

Punctuation and Sentences

1. Try to sum up in a sentence why you need to punctuate your writing.
....

2. Identify five instances where you would need a capital letter.
....

3. Correct the following sentences by putting in capital letters where they are necessary:
   jemma read *Great Expectations* for her english course-work. she had never read charles dickens before; she may read another onc of his novels before easter.
....

4. Identify four of the five punctuation marks that can complete a sentence.
....

5. Explain one of the uses that semi-colons can serve.
....

6. What is a rhetorical question?
....

7. Identify one use for colons.
....

8. Give three of the four rules of direct speech.
....

9. What are the two main purposes of apostrophes?
....

10. Where does the apostrophe need to go with plural nouns that do not need an 's' to make them plurals?
....

11. Identify three of the four types of sentences.
....

12. Point out the main and dependent clauses of this sentence:
    I will go to see the new movie at the cinema as soon I have done the washing up.
....

Spelling and Expression

13. Point out two methods of learning tricky spellings.
....

14. What is before 'e' except after 'c'?
....

15. Why do the following plurals end in 'ies'?
    twenties, lorries, cities, injuries and berries.
....

16. Why do the following plurals end in 's'?
    journeys, trolleys, donkeys, chimneys, toys.
....

17. Which words are American spellings and which are British?
    centre, tyre, theater, humor, cancelled.
....

18. Correct the following spellings:
    begginning, apperance, intrested, grammer, tonge, definately, neccesity, rythm, sentance.
....

19. What are synonyms?
....

20. Why are homophones confusing?
....

21. What are connectives?
....

22. What is the purpose of connectives in writing?

....

23. Why is it necessary to use paragraphs?

....

24. What is a topic sentence?

....

25. Briefly explain what 'control' means in writing.

....

26. Reduce this circumlocution to one word: 'on the grounds that'.

....

Speaking and Listening

27. How many orals do you need to do?

....

28. What must each of them be?

....

29. What is dialect?

....

30. Identify three dialects that can be found in Britain.

....

31. Briefly explain what is meant by standard English.

....

32. When, where and to whom would you use standard English and your local dialect?

....

33. Identify two things that you should keep a note of once you have given your oral in class.

....

34. Briefly explain what is meant by 'body language'.

....

35. What is 'register' in speech?

....

36. Explain what is meant by 'irony'.

....

37. Why is it important to listen?

....

38. What does the word 'analyse' mean?

....

39. What kinds of assignments are suitable for discussing, arguing and persuading?

....

40. Why is it important that you do not write out long passages for your talk?

....

41. What is meant by 'structure' in a talk?

....

42. Why is it important to self-assess after your talk?

....

How did you do?

1–10	correct	start again
11–20	correct	getting there
21–32	correct	good work
33–42	correct	excellent

29

ORIGINAL WRITING (EN3)

WHAT YOU ARE EXPECTED TO DO

Your task is to produce a piece of writing that either <u>explores</u>, <u>imagines</u> or <u>entertains</u> for one or more specific audiences. (Your piece could include all the criteria.)

- In this section you will be assessed on the **<u>quality</u>** of your writing and not on the texts that you have read. There is a wide range of possibilities of what you may write about because there are no restrictions on <u>form,</u> <u>content</u> or <u>genre</u>.

- The exam boards do not usually specify any particular **length** for your work in terms of words or pages; however most of them think that around <u>1000</u> <u>words</u> should be long enough for an accurate assessment of your work to be made. For example, if you submitted a group of poems and wrote a brief account of their composition that would be fine; but long, wordy, unfocused projects are not wanted. What is most important is that the written piece has <u>clear</u> <u>aims</u>, a <u>specific</u> <u>purpose</u>, a <u>particular</u> <u>audience</u> and that it is <u>effectively</u> <u>written</u>. If your work is <u>convincing</u> and <u>concise</u> then the examiner must give it a high mark.

- Teachers are conscious of the **limited time** available to cover both course-work and exam elements of the GSCE. Sometimes they try to cover two or more parts of your course-work using the same topic. For instance, it is not unusual for a media assignment on the comparison of two soaps to extend to a group-oral presentation on a new soap opera. Each member of the group might then go on to produce a piece of original writing by composing a short episode of their soap opera. <u>Media</u> <u>assignments</u> can lend themselves to such creative results.

Examiner's Top Tip
When you produce drafts of your work leave an empty line between each line of text. This will allow you to proof-read more easily, and you can always pencil corrections in the blank lines.

INTERNET
Web sites for examples of excellent stories:
http://164.106.182.10:276/serfweb/phillips/
common/webdocs/ClassicStorylinks.hmtl
http://mbhs.bergtraum.k12.ny.us/cybereng/shorts/
http://www.short-stories.co.uk/

- **If you do not like writing stories you could write an extra chapter for a novel or a scene from a play that you have read. You could, perhaps, write a few diary entries from any major character that impressed you from the texts in your course-work. However, check first that diaries fill the grading criteria for pieces of course-work for your GCSE in Literature.**

WHAT YOU CAN WRITE ABOUT

Here are a few suggested tasks that you could choose from for a fictional piece of writing of 1000 words or so for a story; obviously you would use fewer words for poetry.

Produce a few poems or a long poem such as a ballad to retell an interesting story from the news. Read a few ballads such as *The Lady of Shallot* or *The Ballad of Frankie and Johnny* to get an idea of the form and the effect you can gain from repeating lines and using rhyme in quatrains (four-line stanzas). Notice the rhythm and tone of ballads – in other words, how they sound when read aloud. Could you choose words which would give your poem an appropriate rhythm and tone?

Devise a soap opera and explain the rationale behind its setting, characters, plots and envisaged audience.

Write an extra chapter for a novel.

Write a short horror story with a 'twist in the tale'.

Write an episode or a few detailed scenes for a soap opera.

Write detailed descriptions of people and places with the aim of entertaining and amusing your audience.

Write a one-act play.

Keep an imaginary diary.

HOW YOU WILL BE GRADED

To achieve a good grade from C to A* you will need to:

- write in the appropriate manner for the genre and purpose of your story.

- use a varied range of sentences and vocabulary to keep your audience's interest.

- keep punctuation accurate and produce logical paragraphs to make your meaning clear.

- develop characters and settings within your narrative.

- use literary devices such as similes and metaphors effectively.

- show assured control in your writing with a wide range of expression to achieve effects.

- show an awareness of tone in words and sentences.

- be almost faultless in punctuation and spelling.

- write with flair and originality.

- show that you can be elaborate or concise.

INTERNET

If you would like to read an excellent story with an ingenious ending read **Liam O'Flaherty's** *The Sniper*.

You can find it at:
http://mbhs.bergraum.k12.ny.us/cybereng/shorts/sniper.hmtl

This story has a very short time-frame: its action takes place over a few hours. You could do the same in your story by writing about a single incident or an episode that lasts for only a few hours.

Here are a few titles to get you going if you are stuck for ideas:
'My Last Day on Earth'
'Strange Meeting'
'Emergency on Alpha Minor'
'Danger in Venice'
'The Visitors'
'A Day in my Life as a Dog'

Examiner's Top Tip
Remember that this work is also a dry run for the exam essay. Each piece of writing will need a plan, no matter how brief.

HOW TO WRITE AND PLAN A STORY

PLANNING

Brainstorm or _mind-map your ideas on a blank sheet of paper_. **Sometimes stories can come from _a character_; sometimes they can come from _a specific situation_ such as a shipwreck or a sudden discovery. Once you have a few ideas, try to think of a _title_ because this may help you focus on the _plot_ and _characterisation_ of your story.**

The plot is the plan or outline of your story.
What will be the _climax_ of your plot when your story reaches a crisis? What will be the result of the _climax_? From whose _point of view_ is the story going to be told? Decide if the style of narration is to be in the _first_ or _third person_. _A first-person narrator tells the story from within the story; a third-person narrator stands outside the story_. How much will your narrator know and see? Will the third-person narrator be able to know everything that the characters are thinking? These are matters of _perspective_. _Will the narrator be biased or objective in their viewpoint_?

CHARACTERS

You will need a _main character_ and _two or three_ other important characters. You could include some minor ones, too. Create a brief _profile_ for each character, as this will enable you to be realistic in your portrayal of them. _Have a checklist for each one_, for example, their age, appearance, habits, job, traits, ambitions, hobbies, likes and dislikes, motivation, etc.

SETTING

Where is the story going to be _set_? _Will it be set at home or abroad_? Is the story going to be set in the _present, future or past_? Will your story be drawn from everyday life? Perhaps you would prefer a fairy-tale setting drawn from your imagination? How are you going to describe the setting? Will you suggest the _setting_ as you write with minor details or will you be more elaborate in the details that you give to describe the setting? If necessary do a little research to make your setting _convincing_.

GENRE

Choose a _genre_ for your story. Is your story going to be an adventure, detective, love, science-fiction or comedy story? Can you be even more specific within your _genre_ by going for a sub-division within it (for instance, _comedy-romance_)?

STRUCTURE

Ensure that you have a clear beginning, middle and end in your story. You need to bait your story with a good _'hook'_ at the beginning to make your readers read on. Perhaps you could begin in the middle of an exciting incident; you could use some unusual description or maybe start from an unusual perspective to intrigue the reader. Look at examples in stories you read.

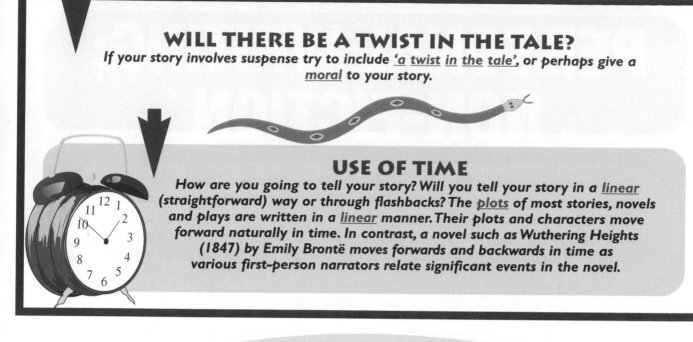

WILL THERE BE A TWIST IN THE TALE?

If your story involves suspense try to include '<u>a twist in the tale</u>', or perhaps give a <u>moral</u> to your story.

USE OF TIME

How are you going to tell your story? Will you tell your story in a <u>linear</u> (straightforward) way or through flashbacks? The <u>plots</u> of most stories, novels and plays are written in a <u>linear</u> manner. Their plots and characters move forward naturally in time. In contrast, a novel such as Wuthering Heights (1847) by Emily Brontë moves forwards and backwards in time as various first-person narrators relate significant events in the novel.

PERSONAL WRITING: FICTION AND THE IMAGINATION (EN3)

QUICK TEST

1. How is a first-person narrative told?

2. What does the term 'genre' mean?

3. What do you need at the beginning of a story to keep your readers interested in reading further?

4. What does it mean to be elaborate?

5. How can you make your characters believable?

Examiner's Top Tip
Remember that the last part of your sentence usually carries most impact so recast your sentences to maximise your impact, in order to give a powerful account of something imagined.

Examiner's Top Tip
Try to use a few literary devices such as similes, metaphors and alliteration in your writing to create effects.

1. By a character in the story, using 'I'.
2. A kind of writing. For example, detective stories, romance, science-fiction, etc.
3. An interesting 'hook' which will seize the attention of an audience.
4. It means going into detail or extensive description.
5. Build up a profile for them; try to give them realistic speech.

PERSONAL WRITING: NON-FICTION

This means writing to: describe, explain, inform, instruct, entertain, report, review, persuade, witness, compare/contrast, request, complain and express feelings. A piece of writing like this could be submitted as course-work. You will definitely be asked to produce more pieces of writing like this in your exam.

WHAT YOU CAN WRITE ABOUT

an <u>autobiographical</u> piece about, say, a memorable trip or holiday that you made with your family; look at magazines which have 'A Day in the Life of Someone'. In some descriptive detail write about a day in your of life for a young person's magazine. <u>Think</u> <u>about</u> <u>your</u> <u>audience</u> <u>as</u> <u>you</u> <u>write</u> <u>your</u> <u>piece</u>. Only you can write about your life so write it as well as you can!

a <u>topic</u> <u>that</u> <u>interests</u> <u>you</u>; explain the issue and give your view of it.

an <u>interesting</u> <u>picture</u> from a newspaper or a magazine; write about it in as much detail as you can.

THIS COULD BE:

a piece of writing in which you give <u>your</u> <u>view</u> on any subject, for example animal experimentation.

a <u>discursive</u> (<u>digressive</u>) essay about two sides of a topical issue in the news.

HOW YOU WILL BE GRADED

Examiner's Top Tip
Always consider the purpose, message, audience and the best form for your writing.

To achieve grades C to A* you will need to:
- <u>research</u> your chosen topic carefully.
- show that your writing is <u>organised</u> and <u>appropriate</u> for your topic.
- <u>interest</u> your readers and sustain points.
- use an appropriate <u>range</u> <u>of</u> <u>punctuation</u> to make your meaning clear.
- be as <u>interesting</u> and <u>original</u> as you can.
- use your <u>own</u> <u>words</u>.
- give a <u>powerful</u> account of a real experience.
- show both <u>elaboration</u> and <u>conciseness</u> in your writing.
- use <u>appropriate</u> <u>registers</u>; that is, match your <u>tone</u> and <u>language</u> to your <u>audience</u>.
- use <u>wide-ranging</u> <u>vocabulary</u> in which <u>syntax,</u> <u>spelling</u> and <u>punctuation</u> <u>is</u> <u>almost</u> <u>faultless</u>.
- consciously <u>shape</u> <u>and</u> <u>craft</u> <u>language</u> to achieve <u>sophisticated</u> <u>effects</u>.
- use <u>standard</u> <u>written</u> <u>forms</u> in a <u>convincing</u> manner.
- produce a <u>well-organised</u> and <u>compelling</u> piece of work.

When grading your work examiners will take into account that you had more time to prepare and present your course-work and will understand that you have limited time in exams.

PLANNING

NON-FICTION WRITING PLAN

Decide on a topic and think about your target audience. The form of writing that you choose will be determined by the type of audience that you want to reach.

Think of an appropriate form: an article, essay, letter, etc.

Do the research: see experts who know the topic; go to libraries; use the Internet; look in encyclopedias; write to associated organisations.

Make notes on one side of pieces of paper and number the pages. Make a mind-map if you prefer. Instructions on how to produce a mind-map and an example are on pages 58–59.

Look over your notes and plan your piece of writing on a single sheet. Number your points. Again this could be organised as a brainstorm.

Remember to write your title when you write or type your first draft. If you hand-write your work leave every second line blank for proof-reading and alterations; it is easier to check your work that way. Always proof-read your work for spelling, punctuation and expression. Read the relevant pages in this book for advice.

Produce your best draft and remember to proof-read your work again for the errors that you are likely to make.

QUICK TEST

1. Identify a form of writing suitable for persuasive writing.
2. What does 'discursive' mean?
3. What is it that you are doing when you look over your work again?
4. How many drafts should you make of your work?
5. Identify three places where you could find information for your chosen topic.

5. Libraries, encyclopedias, the Internet, knowledgeable people, associated organisations.
4. At least two
3. Proof-reading
2. Rambling or digressive – passing from one subject to another.
1. Leaflet or an article on an issue.

HOW TO WRITE ESSAYS

Tips on how to get top marks when writing essays

1 PLANNING

- Examine <u>key</u> <u>words</u> and <u>phrases</u> in the question to help you focus on your answer.
- Read through your notes and any <u>important</u> <u>passages</u> in your text <u>for</u> <u>evidence</u>.
- <u>Brainstorm</u> an essay plan with your essay question in the middle of a blank piece of paper.
- <u>Aim</u> <u>for</u> <u>three</u> <u>or</u> <u>four</u> <u>main</u> <u>arguments</u> and group your points around them. Remember to include page numbers for any <u>quotations</u> used because you will need <u>evidence</u> <u>from</u> <u>your</u> <u>text(s)</u> to prove your <u>arguments</u>.

2 WRITING AN INTRODUCTION

Model introductions

Sometimes it is hard to start essays. A good way to begin is to answer the question briefly in your opening paragraph. Look at your notes and mind-maps to help you.

Example – An Essay Question for *Educating Rita*

Re-read the early and last scenes of *Educating Rita.* Explain what Rita gains and loses in her determination to become educated.

Educating Rita by Willy Russell tells the story of 'Rita' White, a 26-year-old hairdresser, who is trying to 'find herself'. Rita's 'gains' can be summed up as follows:....

The best place for your paragraph on historical context is shortly after your introduction; however it can come anywhere in the essay. This paragraph should be introduced like this:
'Rita is representative of many women in Britain in the late 1970s and 1980s who wanted to live fuller lives. They wanted the greater independence and real choices that could only be achieved through getting an education. However, Rita's experiences show that there were a number of obstacles that women had to face...'

3 THE MAIN BODY OF YOUR ESSAY

☆ Work through <u>each</u> <u>main</u> <u>argument</u> from your introduction as <u>fully</u> as you can.

☆ Once you think that you have proved an argument sufficiently, move on to your next argument. Do <u>not</u> hammer away at the same point for too long.

☆ Remember that your technique must be: <u>point</u>, <u>evidence</u> <u>and</u> <u>comment</u>.

☆ Use a wide range of <u>connective</u> <u>words</u> to link your points and arguments together. (See the spread on connective words on pages 20–21.) These words will join up your points and arguments and link your essay together; the skilful use of <u>connectives</u> can help the <u>fluency</u> <u>of</u> <u>arguments</u> in essays and make them easier to read.

Examiner's Top Tip
Get an idea of what good essays look like. Ask your teacher for good examples of work by former pupils.

4 CONCLUSION

Your essay needs to embody a sense of <u>finality</u>. This should be reflected in the tone of your conclusion.

Conclude by <u>summing</u> <u>up</u> your <u>arguments</u> and <u>findings</u>.

It may be that you have found an alternative way of understanding the question.

Maybe you will have discovered something that needs more <u>research</u>.

It is important to explain what you <u>learned</u> from writing your essay. Give <u>your</u> <u>views</u> on the <u>text(s)</u> that you are writing about.

Examiner's Top Tip
When you begin your essay do not put things off. We often find reasons not to write by doing almost anything else. Get started and fill up those blank pages! You can always correct and improve your work later on.

QUICK TEST

1. What should you focus on in essay questions?

2. What does 'text' mean?

3. What does a text's 'historical context' mean?

4. How many main arguments should you aim for?

5. Where do you give your personal opinion in an essay?

1. Understanding the whole question and paying attention to key words and phrases.   2. Any <u>book</u>, play or poem in any genre.
3. The period in which the text was written and what was going on at the time.   4. Three or four.   5. At the end and nowhere else.

THE MEDIA

NEAB sets a course-work assignment on the media. All the exam boards include questions on a published form of the media in the final exams.

TERMS TO WORK INTO YOUR WRITING ON NEWSPAPERS

Earn higher grades by including these terms in your comments

- **Break**: when the story emerges. Sometimes this is called 'breaking news'.
- **Byline**: gives the name of the journalist who wrote the piece.
- **Caption**: words which explain pictures or artwork.
- **Column**: a vertical article that appears on a page. This can be known as a 'leg'.
- **Copy**: written material submitted for publishing to the editor.
- **Diary column**: either a gossip column or a day-to-day personal column.
- **Down-page**: a name given to a story which appears in the bottom half of a newspaper page.
- **Editorial**: this can be all non-advertising copy. It can also be a column in which the newspaper expresses its opinion on a topic.
- **Exclusive**: a story carried by only one newspaper.
- **Eye-witness reporting**: where the reporter has been at an event.
- **Feature**: a distinct news story. This will give more background information from a wider range of resources than an eyewitness report. The journalist's opinion will be more apparent too.

- **Filler**: a short story of one or two paragraphs, used to fill space when a long story runs short.
- **Hard news**: news which looks at 'who', 'what', 'where', 'when' and 'why'. It is based on factual details with only a little description, journalistic comment or analysis.
- **Human interest story**: this concentrates on tragedy, success, failure, or someone's emotional or sexual history.
- **In-depth reporting**: covers issues in some detail.
- **Lead**: the main story on the page. If this appears on the front page it is sometimes known as a 'splash'.
- **Punch-line**: the main point of a story.
- **Running story**: a story carried over several editions or days.
- **Soft news**: a light news story that is more colourful, witty and carries more commentary than hard news.
- **Tots**: is short for 'Triumph Over Tragedy Story'. These are popular as a human-interest stories.

Examiner's Top Tip
Find out what the word 'text' means and use the term in your writing.

LAYOUT AND PRESENTATION

Below are some useful definitions.
- Artwork: all illustrations, such as cartoons, charts or maps.
- Banner: a front-page headline which spans the top of the page.
- Breaker: any device that breaks up text on a page, such as a cross-head or panel.
- Broadsheet: a larger newspaper often referred to as a 'quality' paper, such as *The Guardian* and *The Times*, aimed at an educated audience.
- Centre-spread: copy (written material) and pictures running over the middle pages of a newspaper.
- Classified ads: small adverts classified according to subject area and without illustrations.
- Colour: for sections of the paper printed on coloured paper such as finance. This can also be used to highlight the views of a journalist or simply descriptions or impressions.

- Crop: to cut a picture down.
- Cross-head: a small heading, normally of one or two words within a text that is often in a larger size of type.
- Display ads: large adverts often with illustrations; they can appear on the editorial pages.
- Layout: the design and look of the page.
- Masthead: the newspaper's title at the top of this page.
- Mug shot: a photo just showing a person's face and sometimes their shoulders.
- Tabloid newspapers: refers to the smaller size of papers like *The Mirror, The Sun* or *The Express*.

HOW YOU WILL BE GRADED

You will be assessed on your ability to read and understand texts (including advertisements, articles, scripts for film, television and radio and any printed material published by the media) <u>as</u> <u>well</u> <u>as</u> <u>write</u> <u>about</u> <u>them</u>. You should aim to:

- express your <u>ideas</u>, <u>opinions</u> and <u>attitudes</u> as <u>impersonally</u> as you can. For example, use 'It seems', or 'the character appears' . . .rather than 'I think', etc. Remember to use the personal pronoun 'I' for what you think only at the end of essays.
- give <u>detailed</u> ideas and points of view.
- show that you can make <u>fine</u> <u>distinctions</u> between points of view.
- <u>analyse</u> (unravel) points in texts as you discuss them.
- show how <u>language</u> is used in media texts.
- make <u>sustained</u> and <u>detailed</u> points on the effectiveness of layout in texts.
- apply <u>appropriate</u> media terms effectively for your chosen text.
- <u>compare</u> media texts.

WHAT YOU WILL BE EXPECTED TO DO

For your coursework assignment you will be expected to **analyse, review** and **comment** on features of a media text such as magazines, radio, television programmes and films. Suitable tasks could include:

- an **examination of a news event** and an analysis of attitudes and bias in the way the news event is reported in different sections of the media such as television, radio and newspapers.

- a written account of a practical activity in which you explain how you made a film, radio interview/show, or produced the front page for a newspaper.

- comparing and contrasting **two soap operas from different countries**.

- analysing a full-page glossy advertisement from a magazine or newspaper.

- planning and producing **a television advert for a product such as a children's toy**.

A FRAMEWORK FOR LOOKING AT TEXTS

To make your analysis, ask the following questions:

<u>Who</u> <u>speaks</u> <u>this</u> <u>text</u>?
- Who is the 'I' or 'we' in the text?

<u>Who</u> <u>is</u> <u>the</u> <u>intended</u> <u>audience</u>?
- Who is expected to hear or read the text?

<u>What</u> <u>kind</u> <u>of</u> <u>text</u> <u>is</u> <u>it</u>?
- Does the text have a recognisable form, such as an article or a leaflet?

<u>What</u> <u>does</u> <u>the</u> <u>text</u> <u>want</u>?
- <u>What</u> <u>are</u> <u>the</u> <u>writer's</u> <u>intentions</u>?
Are the purposes openly stated? What is the expected response?

<u>What</u> <u>does</u> <u>the</u> <u>text</u> <u>mean</u> <u>to</u> <u>me</u>?
- <u>What</u> <u>are</u> <u>my</u> <u>motives</u> for reading it?
How have I understood the text?

<u>Do</u> <u>I</u> <u>share</u> <u>its</u> <u>values</u>?
- What has it made me think about?

Examiner's Top Tip
When you study a media text remember that you are being assessed on your reading as well as your writing skills.

QUICK TEST

1. What is a centre-spread in a newspaper?
2. What is 'hard news'?
3. What is a running story?
4. Who might be the audience for a broadsheet?
5. What is a tabloid?
6. What are the 'classifieds'?

6. Small adverts that are classified according to subject area.
5. A smaller-format newspaper like *The Sun*.
4. An educated audience.
3. A story that runs for days in several editions.
2. Factual news, with little description, comment or analysis.
1. Copy. **Written material and pictures running over the middle pages of a newspaper.**

HOW TO ANALYSE, REVIEW AND COMMENT ON A MEDIA TEXT (EN2/3)

Examiner's Top Tip
Always consider the purpose and target audience of a text before deciding on how its message is driven home.

- Only the best writers of English are hired to write the persuasive letters and information leaflets that pop through your letterbox. What follows are some of the clever ways they persuade or inform us.
- Use junk mail or an information leaflet from your doctor's waiting room or the public library and assess how something is explained or how you are persuaded to part with your money. Find examples of how advertisers try and inform or persuade you in media texts and write about them in a logical way. Try to say something about language first and then layout.

USE OF LANGUAGE TO PERSUADE OR INFORM

- Alliteration and exaggeration are often found in adverts and newspaper headlines. Writers use this to make something sound really enticing or awful. For example, 'Best-Ever Sale Starts Saturday'.

- Boxes are another helpful way of making information accessible.

- Bullet points do the same job: they also give the impression of being evidence; bullet points can also make complex information easy to understand.

- Emotive language is language which tries to get the reader to feel a particular emotion. Comparisons in writing that involve imagery can be surprisingly persuasive. 'For Lydia, life began on the scrap heap . . .' Look out for similes and the metaphor in the example.

- Informal language is made up of casual or shortened words which help create a chatty, friendly tone: 'info', 'sorted', 'nifty', 'piccies', 'mate' etc. This can also include local dialect: 'Watcha mate!'; 'ow's it goin'?'

- Interviews or personal accounts. The personal angle often helps us understand issues in ways that a general account will not. Newspapers and charities know that they can touch and persuade us with personal accounts of an experience: 'Jill lived in a cardboard box for two years.' This is because these organisations know that most people can empathise with the suffering of a single person or a family far better than with that of many thousands of people. News organisations and charities know that we are far more capable of understanding the particular rather than the abstract. Quotations also come into this category when given as evidence.

- Lists of facts also help us to understand the issues. They help support the pleader's case.

- Personal testimony from the famous or experts helps sell products. If David Ginola recommends you use Head and Shoulders, why shouldn't you?

- Questions are used to make you think; sometimes they are rhetorical questions to which no direct answer is expected: 'Now how could you object to that?'

- Repetition is the repeated words or phrases which emphasise a message. 'Fact: there are x number of homeless. Fact: 50 per cent are under the age of x.'

- Slogans can be titles to articles. They are usually catchy and memorable. They can play on well-known catch phrases. For example, 'A dog is for life', 'Cruelty to Children Must Stop!' and 'It's good to talk'.

- The use of the friendly second person such as 'You' or 'Dear Friend' and 'Dear Homeowner'. Look out for a signature at the end of any letters; this is meant as a personal touch and is sometimes in a different colour for extra effect.

PRESENTATION – LAYOUT TO PERSUADE OR INFORM

- **CAPITAL LETTERS CAN BE USED TO HIGHLIGHT IMPORTANT POINTS.**

- <u>Graphs</u> and <u>diagrams</u> make difficult information easy to grasp, especially comparisons, and they also break up forbidding blocks of writing.

- <u>Headings</u> are always important and are often well thought out; watch out for <u>alliteration</u> or <u>similes</u> and <u>metaphors</u> used to drive home points or messages. Here are a few <u>headlines</u> that should never have made it past their editors.

CAUSE OF AIDS FOUND – SCIENTISTS

THUGS EAT AND ROB PROPRIETOR!

Crack found in Australia

- **<u>Fonts</u>** and <u>colours</u> are always carefully chosen. Think about what is implied by the <u>fonts</u> and <u>colours</u> in <u>adverts</u> and <u>logos</u>. Look carefully at packaging, such as a cornflakes packet, and try to detect any subtle messages meant to reinforce public perceptions of the product.

- ***Italics*** *usually identify and emphasise crucial pieces of information.*

- <u>Logos</u> <u>are</u> <u>symbols</u> which represent and identify a company or charity. They can evoke strong messages or ideas and are usually very well thought out.

S

- <u>Maps</u> are useful for finding venues such as tourist attractions.

- <u>Catchy</u> <u>paragraph</u> <u>headings</u> summarise important information immediately in case you do not read the entire piece. They can also persuade you to read on.

- <u>Pictures</u> and <u>images</u> bring texts to life. A well-chosen picture of a child or an animal can tug at your heart-strings and <u>persuade</u> you to give money. Pictures also help break up blocks of writing and invite the reader to linger and find meaning.

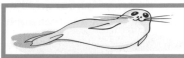

- <u>Captions</u> help us understand pictures and interpret the images in the way the advertiser wants us to.

- <u>The</u> <u>use</u> of <u>colour</u> <u>in</u> <u>pictures</u> <u>and</u> <u>text</u> can reinforce messages and feelings about what you are reading. **Black** is the colour for death and seriousness, **white** is the colour for purity. **Red** is a warm, passionate colour as well as the colour for danger. **Blue** is a cold colour and it evokes the sea or freshness. Look again at your packets of washing powder and at the packaging of grocery items that you may never have consciously thought about before. There is usually a reason for the colours and fonts used on each of them.

- <u>Underlining is another way of emphasising a point and influencing the reader</u>.

QUICK TEST

1. What is the purpose of an advert from a charity?
a) to entertain b) inform/persuade c) evaluate?
2. How do writers create an informal tone?
3. What is emotive language?
4. What is the 'second person' in texts?
5. Why do writers from the media use graphs and diagrams?
6. What is the descriptive comment under a picture called?

1. To inform/persuade.
2. They use abbreviated and informal language or dialect.
3. Language meant to evoke feelings in readers, probably using metaphors and similes.
4. 'You', 'Dear Friend' etc.
5. To break down information to make it easier to understand.
6. A caption.

HOW TO BEGIN YOUR ESSAY

CHOOSE YOUR ADVERT

- <u>Choose</u> <u>an</u> <u>interesting,</u> <u>colourful,</u> <u>full-page</u> <u>advert</u> <u>from</u> <u>a</u> <u>magazine</u> and work out how the advertisers persuade their target audience to buy their product. How do they get their message across and how successful are they in doing so?
- Tick the points that apply to your chosen advert and work through the points as fully as you can.

YOUR ESSAY TITLE

The following information should be included in the title of your media essay:
- the name of the product
- the name of the advertiser or maker of the product
- the name and date of the magazine or newspaper where you found the advert.

A typical essay title could be worded as follows:

An analysis of a magazine advert for a Vaio laptop by Sony. The product was advertised in *The Observer Life Magazine* on 25 February 2001.

INTRODUCTION

Explain briefly what you are going to write about:
- the main subject(s) of the advert; that is the product and any models associated with it
- the advertisement's layout; that is, the overall appearance of the advert on the page
- the persuasive techniques used in the advert
- the intended target audience of the advert.

Examiner's Top Tip
Use standard English in formal essays. Avoid dialect unless it is called for.

WHO IS THE TARGET AUDIENCE FOR THE ADVERT?

- **Who is the advert aimed at? Give their age, sex, class, lifestyle, etc. The target audience will have a major influence on how the advert is set out and promoted.**

DESCRIBE THE MAIN SUBJECTS OF THE ADVERT

- *Examine the <u>status</u> and <u>appearance</u> of the product and the models that are associated with it.*

- *<u>Give</u> <u>details</u> about the main model's age, clothing, style, hair, etc. Examine the body language of the models (their facial expressions, eye contact, activity, pose, etc.).*

- *<u>What</u> <u>is</u> <u>the</u> <u>photographic</u> <u>coding</u> <u>of</u> <u>the</u> <u>advert</u>? (This refers to its framing, focus, angle, shading, effects and lighting.) Most adverts are <u>back-lit</u>; but other important strong lights include <u>key</u> and <u>filler</u> <u>lights</u> which are positioned to the side of the* camera. These lights are usually trained on the models or on the product to make them appear bright and to avoid shadows. Think about the effects that can occur when one or more of these lights are switched off from the front, rear or side. For example, a shaded part of the advert would give a mysterious tone or feel to the advert and this would be a deliberate effect. *<u>Lighting</u> is often used to create <u>mood</u> and <u>atmosphere</u>.*

- *<u>Examine</u> <u>any</u> <u>objects</u> <u>in</u> <u>the</u> <u>advert</u> and look just as carefully at the <u>background</u>. What do you think is the <u>purpose</u> of any <u>objects</u> or <u>signs</u> which may be in the <u>background</u> of the advert? Companies spend a lot of money on these adverts. Nothing is there by chance!*

- *The <u>context</u> (where and when) of the advert. Where does the advert fit in with the magazine in which it appears? What kind of story does it appear beside? Is there a link with an article? Does it allude to a topical event? Is the advert set in the present, future or past?*

DESCRIBE THE ADVERT'S LAYOUT

- Think about the use of <u>colour</u>. What do the colours used suggest? Has colour any <u>symbolic</u> <u>significance</u> in the advert?

- Comment on any other <u>graphic devices</u> that are present in your chosen advertisement. Suggest why they are there.

- How is <u>space</u> used within the advert? Does the model or product fill all the available space? Why or why not? What might be suggested by <u>empty spaces</u>?

- What is the <u>typography</u> of the advert? That is, the use of <u>type size</u>, <u>type style</u>, <u>fonts</u> etc.

A MEDIA ESSAY TO ANALYSE AN ADVERT (EN2/3)

This will show you how to analyse an advert from a magazine. It could also help you catch up with your course-work or improve on an earlier media assignment.

ASSESS YOUR ADVERT'S PERSUASIVE TECHNIQUES

- its <u>genre</u> and <u>conventions</u>. In other words, what types of people are shown and <u>how</u> <u>are</u> <u>they</u> <u>presented</u>? Is the scene filled with secret agents, business people, pop stars, gamblers, etc. or does the advert try to recreate romantic or thrilling scenes, Victorian times, modern living or the future? <u>How</u> <u>is</u> <u>the</u> <u>chosen</u> <u>genre</u> <u>persuasive</u>?

- any <u>celebrities</u> or <u>personalities</u> used and what they are normally associated with. Does the advertised product feed off <u>any</u> <u>associations</u> with these celebrities?

- any <u>hard</u> <u>information</u>: facts, figures, etc.

- promises of <u>pleasure</u>. What good things could result from buying the product?

Write about any of the following that apply to your advert

- any <u>figures</u> <u>of</u> <u>speech</u>, including puns or double meanings, personification, alliteration, etc.

- any sense of <u>belonging</u>: are you expected to identify with any group, class, trend, etc.?

- <u>expert</u> <u>witnesses</u> or <u>personal</u> <u>testimony</u> and what is gained from their use.

- <u>scientific</u> <u>jargon</u>: unusual words and terms that are meant to impress <u>an</u> <u>audience</u>.

- any appeals to your <u>conscience</u>: emotional blackmail, lifestyle, commitments.

- any <u>advantageous</u> <u>promises</u>: freebies, coupons, improved lifestyle, freedom, sexual attractiveness.

- repetition with the <u>rule</u> <u>of</u> <u>three</u> to help emphasise points.

Examiner's Top Tip
If you get stuck on any of the points for this essay just ask your teacher. That is what he or she is there for.

CONCLUSION

- Say whether you think your chosen advert is <u>successful</u> in its aims. If you think that it was, briefly sum up why. You could recycle the most interesting findings of your essay here.
- Explain what you have <u>learned</u> through writing this essay and <u>give</u> <u>your</u> <u>final</u> <u>views</u> on advertisers and the methods that they use through advertising agencies to persuade us to buy their products.

HOW TO WRITE ABOUT A TV ADVERT (EN2/3)

OTHER POINTS TO CONSIDER ON TV ADVERTS

Look back at the previous spread to see the methods which advertisers use to persuade us on paper. Which of these can be applied to TV adverts?

OTHER CAMERA SHOTS WHICH HELP TELL A STORY

- CUTS: changes of scenes from one setting to another.
- DISSOLVE: where one scene dissolves into another.
- WIPE: where one scene is wiped from the screen by another.
- MONTAGE, otherwise known as 'rapid editing': a number of camera shots that follow each other in quick succession to create an effect. This type of approach is usually used alongside a soundtrack. A good, recent example of this is the stunningly dramatic opening of Romeo and Juliet (1996) starring Leonardo Di Caprio and Clare Danes.
  If you find montage being used in your advert the main question that you need to ask is Why? What is the purpose behind the effect?

MORE STORY-LINE FEATURES TO THINK ABOUT

- The use of narrative to entertain viewers. Is the advert a one-off or one of a series? Either way, what is the storyline of the advert? How does it help sell the product?

- Stereotypes can be used as a means for quick understanding: working/careworn housewives, unattractive traffic wardens, etc. Given the time restrictions on an advert, such use of shorthand for instant understanding is inevitable. Do they help sell the product?

- The choice of setting: workplace, bar, home, market, imaginary, etc. Is the advert set in the present, future or past? Does the setting have any bearing on the persuasiveness of the advert?

- The use of a particular genre: spy, thriller, musical, adventure, romantic comedy, etc. Again, does this sell the product? What persuasive associations can you draw from the advertiser's chosen genre?

- What values seem to be within and outside the adverts? Is there anything in it that we are expected to agree with? Look out for values that suggest 'family life', 'law and order', 'making money', 'being an individual', 'freedom', etc.

- How music and sound are used to create mood and atmosphere. Is the music realistically part of the background, say coming from a jukebox (diagetic sound) or is it deliberately inserted into the advert (non-diagetic sound)? What is the effect of using each type of sound? How does the sound add to the persuasiveness of the advert?

- The use of voice-overs. Voices to endorse products can also help create a mood and atmosphere. The voices can suggest sexually charged women, reassuring males or convincing experts and may be provided by celebrities.

- The use of increased volume. It sometimes seems that the volume goes up on some commercial television channels the instant the adverts come on! Perhaps the advertiser want to ensure that you heard their message even if you have left the room. Advertisers seem to be using this technique more and more.

- Who the target audience could be. This will be determined by when the advert is shown and the programmes shown during commercial breaks and after the advert.

CHOOSE AN ADVERT THAT INTERESTS YOU AND RECORD IT

Examine the **methods** **through** **which** the **advertiser** **tries** **persuade** **you** to **buy** a **product** or **use** a **service**. Look carefully at some television adverts and notice how the **shot-building** occurs. This, taken together with how camera shots are **framed**, is part of the '**grammar**' of film. Much of what follows could be applied to any movie assignments that you have been set.

The usual rule for camera work in television is that there are **no more than two people in a room**. If there are more than two characters in a room then the camera tends to only focus on two of them.

Here are a number of **basic** **terms** to consider when you do your research. Use them as you make points in your essays and show how they add meaning to the **persuasiveness** of an advert.

SHOT-MAKING WITH A CAMERA

Camera shots help tell a story **visually** and they contribute towards **mood** **and** **atmosphere**. They often build up to **close-ups** and then back to **half** **shots** and **total** **shots** as scenes reach a level of **dramatic** **intensity** and then fall away. **You** **could** **have,** **say,** **an** **establishing** **shot,** **two** **total** **shots,** **four** **mid** **shots,** **six** **close-ups** **and** **then** **back** **to** **four** **mid** **shots** **followed** **by** **two** **total** **shots** etc**. It is a bit like composing music.

- **Establishing** shot: this shot locates **time** **and place**. For example if the action switches to an airport, the camera shows us shots of planes landing to tell us that the scene is now at an airport.

- **Long** shot or **total** shot: this shows **the whole body** and lets you know who is important in the advert.

- **Mid** shot: this shows the chest and shoulders. It shows **who is talking** and who is **significant** in a scene.

- **Close-Up**: this is an expressive shot for the director. **It** **can** **show** **emotion** of all kinds. **Extreme** **close-ups** might show only a mouth, for example.

- **Pan** shot: the camera swivels from one thing to another.

- **Pull** **focus**: the depth of field or **background** changes from one character or part of a set to another.

- **Point** **of** **view**: a camera shot from the point of view of a character. This camera shows what a character would see. In other words, the camera substitutes for the character.

- **High-angle** **shots**: these shots tend to look down on someone or a **scene**. They show power for the viewer and vulnerability for the person looked upon. They can be related to the **point** **of** **view** – and thus power – of another **character**. The effect is similar with a **low-angle** **shot** in which a character seems powerless, having to look up at someone above them.

QUICK TEST

1. What is a point-of-view shot?
2. What is an establishing shot?
3. Where would you expect to see an establishing shot in a programme?
4. What emotions can a high-angle shot bring out?
5. What is the ideal number of characters in a scene for television?
6. What is meant by a 'stereotype'?
7. What is the significance of a long shot?

1. The camera shows what a particular character can see.
2. The shot sets the scene and lets the audience know where the action is taking place.
3. At the beginning of a programme and every time a major change of scene happens.
4. A sense of power for the one looking down, vulnerability for anyone looking up.
5. Two (it is an unwritten rule in television)
6. When we see people as types and not as individuals.
7. It introduces the significant characters in a scene.

EXAM QUESTIONS - Use the questions to test your progress. Check your answers on page 94.

Original Writing

1. Will you be assessed on writing or reading?

....

2. What is the word length that you should be aiming at?

....

3. What does 'narrative' mean?

....

4. What does 'genre' mean?

....

5. Similes are comparisons. How do they differ from metaphors?

....

6. What does 'hook' mean in terms of stories?

....

7. What is meant by 'setting'?

....

8. Give two examples of what you could write about as an assignment.

....

9. What does 'original writing' mean?

....

10. What are the main styles of narration?

....

11. If a narrator is outside the story, what is he or she?

....

12. What does 'plot' mean?

....

13. Give a method by which you can plan your story.

....

14. Explain what is meant by 'control' in writing.

....

15. If writing is linear what is it?

....

Personal Writing – Non-Fiction

16. What does non-fiction mean?

....

17. Give two examples of what you could write about.

....

18. If your task is 'discursive' how is it written?

....

19. Give three sources where you could find information on a topic.

....

20. Will an imaginative story be suitable for a non-fiction assignment?

....

21. What does 'target audience' mean?

....

22. Identify three forms that you could use for persuasive writing.

....

23. What is meant by the term 'text'?

....

24. Name a text that 'informs' or 'advises'.

....

25. Is biography a form of non-fiction?

....

26. If you are asked to 'compare' and 'contrast' what are you expected to do?

....

27. What is meant by the 'historical context' of a text?

....

28. Briefly explain what you need to do to write an essay.

....

29. Where do you put your personal views in an essay?

....

30. Explain what 'Point—Evidence —Comment' means.

....

The Media

31. What does the term 'media' include?

....

32. Identify a task that you could do as a media assignment.

....

33. Explain these terms from 'Layout and Presentation':
a) artwork..
b) broadsheet...
c) layout..
d) mug-shot...
e) display ads...

34. Explain these terms from 'Writing and Language' in the media:
a) byline..
b) exclusive..
c) human-interest story...
d) punch-line..
e) lead story...

35. Give three of five questions that you should ask of any non-fiction text.

....

36. Find and give an example of emotive language from a leaflet or advert promoted by a charity.

....

37. What is a slogan? Write down two examples.

....

38. Why do companies create logos?

....

39. Give two examples of how writers use presentation and layout to emphasise their points.

....

40. Give an example of the 'second person'.

....

How did you do?

1–10	correct	....start again
11–20	correct	....getting there
21–30	correct	....good work
31–40	correct	....excellent

WHAT YOU MAY STUDY

This will be determined by what your English teachers have in their stock cupboard; you'll probably get to study what Year 9 have not been set for their Sats! **If you are lucky there will be a recent film of the play** that you can rent which will help your overall understanding of it.

As you read the play try to get **the gist** of what **characters** are saying before you read passages again for a more detailed understanding. Make use of any general notes in your books to guide your understanding as well.

The plays you are most likely to study are:

Antony and Cleopatra   *Macbeth*
Henry IV Part One or Two   *A Midsummer's Night's Dream*
Henry V   *The Tempest*
Julius Caesar   *Twelfth Night*
The Merchant of Venice   *The Winter's Tale*
Romeo and Juliet

Examiner's Top Tip
To understand Shakespeare aim to get a rough idea of what is going on. Once you have this you can then deepen your understanding by reading for more meaning in imagery and word choices. A good exercise to attune yourself to the language is to translate six-line passages into modern English.

THE SHAKESPEARE ASSIGNMENT

HOW YOU WILL BE GRADED

To achieve grades C to A* you will need to show that you are able to do some of the following:

1. You will show through your <u>critical</u> <u>and</u> <u>personal</u> <u>response</u> how meaning is made in the play.

2. You will be expected to support your points with <u>textual</u> <u>evidence</u> on the play's <u>language,</u> <u>themes,</u> <u>characters</u> <u>or</u> <u>structure</u>.

3. You should show that you understand the play and the implications from its <u>themes</u> and <u>relevance</u> for what people thought important in Shakespeare's day and in our time. <u>Interpretations</u> <u>of</u> <u>texts</u> can change over time as people read them in accordance with the <u>values</u> <u>and</u> <u>ideas</u> of their time.

4. In some of your comments you should show an awareness of Shakespeare's <u>linguistic</u> <u>devices</u>: his use of <u>imagery</u> through <u>metaphors,</u> <u>similes,</u> <u>personification,</u> <u>alliteration,</u> <u>oxymorons</u>, etc.

5. Try to say something about the play's <u>philosophical</u> <u>context</u> and how the play sits within its <u>dramatic</u> <u>genre</u>. The <u>philosophical</u> <u>context</u> means the values and ideas that were thought important when the play was written. An hour or two with an up-to-date history book of the time would help you find these things out.

6. You should give <u>detailed</u> <u>and</u> <u>sustained</u> <u>analysis</u> of Shakespeare's use of language for <u>poetic,</u> <u>figurative</u>, and <u>dramatic</u> <u>effect</u> and develop your points.

7. Try, if you can, to show an awareness of <u>alternative</u> <u>interpretations</u> in your writing.

WHAT YOU HAVE TO DO

You will need to show that you <u>understand</u> the play and can engage with it in an essay or a piece of writing.

If your essay or writing is going be used to count for your Literature GCSE you'll also need to show an awareness of <u>the background</u> to the play. That is, the <u>historical, cultural</u> and <u>literary</u> traditions which <u>shaped Shakespeare's play</u>. The best place to include such <u>background</u> is in the early part of your essay.

YOU COULD:

- <u>write an essay on a character, themes</u> or <u>structure</u> of the play
- <u>examine the dramatic qualities</u> of one or more scenes
- <u>write a commentary</u> after hot-seating or role-playing a character from your play
- <u>write a character study</u>
- <u>analyse the dramatic effects of imagery</u> or other language features in the play
- <u>write about a performance of the play</u> from the theatre, television or film.

Examiner's Top Tip
As with any writer, when you write essays on Shakespeare you should use the P.E.C. method:
- make a point
- give evidence for your point
- comment on your evidence.

SHAKESPEARE'S CHOICE OF LANGUAGE

Shakespeare used <u>three styles of writing</u> in his plays. Here are a few examples from **Twelfth Night**:

1. <u>Poetic Verse (Rhymed)</u> Often used to signal the end of scenes like a curtain call or for heightened dramatic effect. Take, for example, this rhyming couplet from Twelfth Night:

Duke Orsino: *Away before me to sweet beds of flowers:*
Love-thoughts lie rich when canopied with bowers.

2. <u>Blank Verse (Unrhymed)</u> Verse which was intended to represent the rhythms of speech.
It is usually used by noble characters who are given elevated speech to show their feelings and mood:

Duke Orsino: *If music be the food of love play on.*

Note how the speech is in <u>iambic pentameter</u>. That is, it has 10 syllables to the line in which five are <u>stressed</u>. The <u>rhythm pattern</u> is ti-tum, ti-tum, ti-tum, ti-tum, ti-tum. Sometimes you'll find more or fewer <u>stresses</u> to the lines yet the overall pattern will be even in the end.

3. <u>Prose</u> Ordinary language used by characters of all ranks. Uneducated characters tend to use it. It can also be used for comic exchanges between characters, for plot development and for speech which lacks dramatic intensity:

Viola as Cesario: *Save thee, friend, and thy music.*
Dost thou live by thy tabor?
Feste: *No, sir, I live by the church*
Viola: *Art thou a churchman?*
Feste: *No such matter sir: I do live by the church;*
for I do live at my house, and my house
doth stand by the church.

Twelfth Night

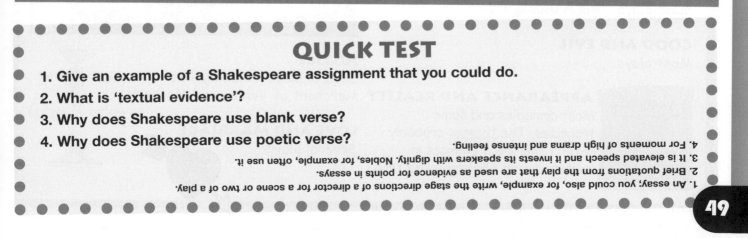

QUICK TEST

1. Give an example of a Shakespeare assignment that you could do.
2. What is 'textual evidence'?
3. Why does Shakespeare use blank verse?
4. Why does Shakespeare use poetic verse?

4. For moments of high drama and intense feeling.
3. It is elevated speech and it invests its speakers with dignity. Nobles, for example, often use it.
2. Brief quotations from the play that are used as evidence for points in essays.
1. An essay; you could also, for example, write the stage directions of a director for a scene or two of a play.

THE STRUCTURE AND THEMES OF SHAKESPEARE'S PLAYS

This typical structure or plot of a Shakespeare play is oversimplified, but this basic framework should help you see how the play that you are studying is set out.

SOME RECURRING THEMES, IDEAS OR MESSAGES

CONFLICT
Macbeth, Julius Caesar, Romeo and Juliet, Antony and Cleopatra, The Merchant of Venice, Henry IV Parts I and II and Henry V.

VARIOUS FORMS OF LOVE AND LOYALTY
Twelfth Night, Romeo and Juliet, A Midsummer Night's Dream, The Merchant of Venice, Antony and Cleopatra and The Winter's Tale.

CHANGE
Characters in most plays. Some characters such as Malvolio (Twelfth Night) and Shylock (The Merchant of Venice), are punished because they cannot change.

FATE
Most plays; also the role of the individual against society.

FORTUNE
Fvery play. This is the notion of the Goddess of Fortune making and breaking us by giving or denying us luck.

ORDER, DISORDER AND STABILITY
Most plays. This is usually linked to Nature.

GOOD AND EVIL
Most plays.

APPEARANCE AND REALITY
Most comedies and some tragedies. The themes probably reflect the great changes in society during Shakespeare's time.

DISGUISE AND IDENTITY
Most comedies and some tragedies. The plays often depict the gap between what is said and how it is interpreted. Characters can deceitfully misuse words too.

SELF-KNOWLEDGE
This can be found in most comedies; however there is often one character, like Malvolio in Twelfth Night, who is incapable of accepting his faults and learning about himself.

KINGSHIP AND THE USE AND ABUSE OF POWER
Macbeth, Julius Caesar, Henry IV Parts I and II and Henry V.

JUSTICE
Several plays including The Merchant of Venice and Macbeth.

LOVE AND MARRIAGE
Several plays.

PLOT STRUCTURE

Shakespeare liked to stress the comedy or seriousness of many scenes within his plays by making <u>dramatic</u> <u>contrasts</u>. He did this by placing <u>a serious scene after a comic one</u> and vice versa.

- <u>Main characters are introduced to the audience</u>. Order reigns and the world and nature are in natural harmony.

- <u>Problems are revealed</u>. Things begin to go wrong. Confusions, murders, deceit, pranks and other complications begin.

- As events progress there is <u>chaos</u> and a <u>loss of order and harmony</u>. The natural world appears out of sorts.

- Things come to a head in the play's <u>climax</u>. (Climax comes from the Greek word for 'ladder'). If you are reading a <u>tragedy</u> then several more deaths occur now, including a main character like Macbeth. <u>The climax is the moment of the highest dramatic intensity</u> in the play, particularly for the main character.

Examiner's Top Tip
Always be prepared to say what you think of the play that you studied. Your view is important and it should be expressed at the end of your essay.

- <u>Order</u> is <u>re-established</u> with the right people in control again. <u>Nature is again at one with the main characters</u>. Comedies usually end in several, usually three, marriages.

QUICK TEST

1. What is a theme?
2. Where would you find the 'climax' of a play?
3. What does 'plot' mean?
4. What does 'context' mean?
5. Why would it be useful to see a performance of a Shakespeare play?

Examiner's Top Tip
Go to see a live performance of a play if you can because this will help your understanding of the play. Shakespeare intended his plays to be performed and not read when he wrote them.

1. It is the play's main message or idea. There can be several themes in a play.
2. Near the end
3. The plan or outline of the play.
4. The events and ideas around at the time when the text was written.
5. It would help you understand the whole play and know how speeches could be interpreted. Shakespeare wanted his plays to be heard and seen, not just read.

SHAKESPEARE'S IMAGERY

FIGURES OF SPEECH

Shakespeare uses <u>figures</u> <u>of</u> <u>speech</u> – that is, <u>imagery</u> or <u>word</u> <u>pictures</u> – to do the following:
- say more about points made in <u>dialogue</u> and <u>action</u>
- <u>reinforce</u> and <u>enhance</u> the <u>audience's</u> <u>ideas</u> of the <u>characters</u>
- <u>magnify</u> or <u>draw</u> <u>attention</u> to <u>themes/issues</u> in the text.

To do this he uses:

- <u>**similes**</u>: comparisons using <u>'as'</u> or <u>'like'</u>: 'The moon is <u>like</u> a balloon.'

- <u>**personification**</u>: giving human feelings to animals or inanimate objects.

  - <u>**metaphors**</u>: stronger comparisons saying some-thing is something else: 'The moon is a balloon.'

- <u>**extended**</u> <u>**metaphors**</u>: a metaphor that is used extensively throughout a passage. <u>See</u> <u>the</u> <u>example</u> opposite on 'roses' and 'women'.

- <u>**oxymorons**</u>: these are <u>words</u> and <u>phrases</u> that you would not expect to see yoked together to cause an effect. As soon as Juliet hears that Tybalt, her cousin, has been killed by Romeo her grief and outrage is tempered by her disbelief that Romeo could carry out such a deed:

'Fiend angelical, dove-feathered raven, wolvish-ravening lamb, ... A damned saint, an honourable villain!'
– *Romeo and Juliet*, Act 3, Scene 2, lines 75–79

- <u>**motifs**</u>: <u>characters,</u> <u>themes</u> <u>or</u> <u>images</u> which <u>recur</u> throughout a text. For example, <u>disguise</u> is a running idea in Twelfth Night. In *Macbeth* there are several <u>motifs</u>. One is <u>'fair</u> <u>and</u> <u>foul'</u> and another is <u>sleep</u>. To the Weird Sisters, who characterise evil, what is ugly is beautiful, and what is beautiful is ugly: 'Fair is foul and foul is fair.' Macbeth and Lady Macbeth reign in restless ecstasy after murdering King Duncan. Macbeth soon says to illustrate the sleep <u>motif</u>:

'Me thought I heard a voice cry, 'Sleep no more!''
Macbeth does murder sleep — the innocent sleep,
Sleep that knits up the ravelled sleave of care,
The death of each day's life, sore labour's bath,
Balm of hurt minds, great nature's second course
Chief nourisher in life's feast.'
– *Macbeth*, Act 2, Scene 2, 34–39

Examiner's Top Tip
If the audience knows more about a development of the plot than the characters then this is known as dramatic irony.

Examiner's Top Tip
Keep quotations relevant and brief. Aim to use single words and phrases or no more than a sentence or so to prove your points. Remember to comment on the quotations that you use: your style should be P.E.C. (point – evidence – comment).

AN EXTENDED EXAMPLE OF SHAKESPEARE'S USE OF IMAGERY

In *Twelfth Night*, Viola as Cesario speaks <u>ironically</u> of her 'concealed' love for the Duke as she tells him about how her 'Father had a daughter loved a man':

'**Duke Orsino:** And what's her history?
Viola: A blank my lord. She never told her love,
But let concealment, like a worm i' the bud
Feed on her damask cheek. She pined in thought,
And with a green and yellow melancholy
She sat like Patience on a monument,
Smiling at grief. Was not this love indeed?
We men may say more, swear more, but indeed
Our shows are more than will; for still we prove
Much in our vows, but little in our love.'
– *Twelfth Night*, Act 2, Scene 4, lines 110–119

- In this moving speech Viola uses two <u>similes</u> to stress her torment. She sees herself as <u>personifying</u> the virtue, Patience. She <u>metaphorically</u> compares her cheek and her womanhood to the red of a 'damask' (rose) in full bloom but through concealment is now dying from grief. She is also comparing concealment to the worm that will destroy the rose. The image recalls the Duke's words and Viola's answer on lines 38–39:

'**Duke Orsino:** For women are as roses, whose fair flower
Being once displayed, doth fall that very hour.
Viola: And so they are; alas, that they are so –
To die, even they to perfection grow.'
Act 2, Scene 4

Examiner's Top Tip
Get a recording of a play from your local library and listen to parts of the play as it is read. It will help your understanding of the play.

QUICK TEST

Circle the correct answer:

1. A theme is:

   a) a song b) an idea/issue or message c) personification d) a character.

2. Shakespeare uses imagery to:

   a) make his writing pretty b) because he is vain c) fill up space d) enhance our understanding of a character, theme or a point.

3. A simile is a figure of speech which:

   a) draws a comparison using 'as' or 'like' b) allows characters to smile c) has to do with singularity d) makes a comparison using 'is' or 'are'?

4. The term 'imagery' means:

   a) looking in mirrors b) word pictures c) writing prose d) knitting.

5. The climax of a play is:

   a) its ending b) its beginning c) when the action comes to a head d) in the middle.

1. b
2. d
3. a
4. b
5. c

FESTE'S ROLE AS A JESTER

Feste is a jester and **his name suggests the festive element in the play** which is named after the 12th day of Christmas, in which servants could play their masters and vice versa.

As Feste was Olivia's father's jester, **he is an older, more experienced figure** in a play, where there are no parents to guide the younger; he helps the audience to understand other characters because he can see what most of them cannot.

He is a **'licensed fool'** in the tradition of **wise fools** who tell their masters and mistresses the truth about themselves. As Olivia says to Malvolio: 'There is no slander in an allowed fool, though he do nothing but rail nor no railing in a known discreet man, though he do nothing but reprove.' Act 1, Scene 5, lines 93–95

He is **an independent character** because he moves between the houses and the characters.
He also remains constant throughout the play. Feste reminds us that anyone, including the audience, can be a fool. When told by Viola that he was seen at Count Orsino's court, he replies: 'Foolery, sir, does walk about the orb like the sun, it shines everywhere.'
Act 3, Scene 1

Feste is a **successful jester.** He is paid for his songs and jests by most of the important characters of the play.

FESTE'S SONGS
The function of his songs is to entertain the characters and audience by telling them the **truth** about themselves through **irony.**

Festes' songs are about **'love' or 'good life'.** The song of 'love', 'O Mistress Mine', is highly **ironic** in that it foretells the coming of the twins, Cesario and Sebastian, to Olivia:
'O mistress mine where are you roaming?
O stay and hear, your true love's coming,
That can sing both high and low'. Act 2, Scene 3

The song ends on a note of *Carpe Diem* ('Seize the day') because 'Youth's a stuff will not endure'. This is almost certainly intended for Sir Toby, Maria and Sir Andrew and perhaps us too.

His final song is a 'Song of Good Life'. It alludes to **realism** and **entertainment** and that the audience can take the play in **'Whatever way it wants to'**; this is also the likely message of **the play's subtitle, 'What You Will'.**

FESTE'S IDEAS ABOUT LANGUAGE

He is concerned about the uses language is made to serve. This is linked to the play's themes of disguise and deception, as well as love

He tells Viola that 'Words have grown false. I am loath to prove reason with them.' Act 3, Scene 1

He also tells Viola that he is not Olivia's 'fool, but her corrupter of words'. Like a glove, he can turn meaning inside out: 'You see the age! A sentence is but a cheveril glove to a good wit; how quickly the wrong side may be turned outward.' Act 3, Scene 1

Feste later thinks that Sebastian's use of the word 'vent' as in 'vent your folly' somewhere else, seems strange from someone of Sebastian's apparent rank and status. Feste taunts Sebastian, 'He has heard that word of some great man and now applies it to a fool.' Act 4, Scene 1

Thus the world for Feste seems turned upside down with people who are not much higher than servants speaking like their masters.

Maria's riddle-like letter, which is made to appear as if it comes from Olivia, is the main example in the play of language being made to serve another purpose: the deception and ridicule of Malvolio.

FESTE ON THE OTHER CHARACTERS

ON VIOLA AS CESARIO

He says that he does not care for Viola, probably sensing her **disguise** and adds:

'If that be to care for nothing sir, I would it would make you invisible.'

Act 3, Scene 1

VIOLA/CESARIO ON FESTE

She sees Feste's fooling as appropriate and notices the 'hawk-like' way that he sees others:

'He must observe their mood on whom he jests, The quality of persons, and the time; And, like the haggard, (hawk) check at every feather That comes before his eye.' Act 3, Scene 1

ON OLIVIA

He is loyal to Olivia and thinks of her as 'My mouse of virtue' ('My good little thing'). He catechises her in order to prove her foolishness for mourning too long over her brother. Act 1, Scene 5

ON MALVOLIO

Feste dislikes his **main antagonist** for his pride and self-love. Feste ironically tells Malvolio soon after encountering him, 'God send you a speedy infirmity, for the better increasing of your folly'. Act 1, Scene 5 Feste has revenge on Malvolio for being called 'a barren rascal' and other put-downs by later pretending to be Sir Topas.

ON DUKE ORSINO

Feste sees him as giddy and 'inconstant' in his feelings. Feste compares him to a sailor on an aimless voyage:

'Now the melancholy god protect thee, and the tailor make thy doublet of changeable taffeta, for thy mind is a very opal. I would have men of such constancy put to sea, that their business might be everything and their intent everywhere.' Act 1, Scene 4

ESSAY NOTES FOR FESTE'S ROLE AND FUNCTION IN *TWELFTH NIGHT*

Examiner's Top Tip
Shakespeare's primary concern is for language! Once you appreciate this you can then get to grips with his outlandish plots.

QUICK TEST

1. What are the main ways in which you can find out about a character?

2. Name the three main types of Shakespeare plays.

3. Why does Shakespeare have important characters speak soliloquies?

1. From what they say, what they do and from what others say about them. You can discover more from any imagery associated with them.
3. Shakespeare mainly wrote history, tragedy and comedy plays.
4. Dramatists wrote soliloquies for important characters to help audiences understand the thoughts, feelings and motives of these characters.

PREPARATIONS

Look carefully at the notes on the previous pages on Feste as they will help you to work your way through this essay. Always write down the title of your essay in your draft as well as the best copy of your essay. This allows you to see whether your points and arguments are relevant; it also helps the teacher/examiner know the case that you are trying to prove and whether you have proved it!

Examiner's Top Tip
In order to get a high mark you will need to include some comments on the cultural and historical context of the play that you have been asked to study.

MAIN BODY OF YOUR ESSAY

- Work your way through the first point and the main arguments in your introduction. Remember to prove what you say by using the point – explain – comment method.

- You will need to write a paragraph or so in which you briefly set out where and when the play was performed (the literary, historical and cultural context). Who would have seen the play, and what would its significance have been for them? Twelfth Night was put on in the Middle Temple Inn of Court before a mixed audience of the royal court and lawyers on 6 January (Twelfth Night) in 1602. This intellectual audience would have appreciated the cleverness of Shakespeare's complex play and also enjoyed the upside-down world that it represents.

- You can try to work comments about context into your essay as you write about the characters and main ideas.

Taking the arguments suggested above, in turn:

1. Explain who Feste is and his comic role and function as jester, singer and truth-teller to the characters and the audience. You could comment on the role of jesters in the Middle Ages and their role or function in Shakespeare's time. You will need to research this background information.

2. Point out his independence within the play; show how he moves between the main settings and how he points out that foolery is 'everywhere'.

3. Show how he has self-knowledge and is able to help an audience understand the main characters and gain an insight into them.

4. Show how Feste views language with mistrust and how language and its misuse can be linked with the play's main themes of love, deception and disguise.

5. Explain that Feste shows us through songs of 'love' and 'good life' that we must seize our happiness when we can because life is short. He reminds us that we have been watching a fantasy and that the play was meant mainly to entertain his early intellectual audience as well as later audiences.

Examiner's Top Tip
Proof-read your essay for punctuation, capital letters and clarity of expression. Remember to check the relevance of your points and arguments. Ask yourself, 'Have I answered the question?'

ESSAY TITLE

The essay title that is being answered here is: **What is the function (role) and significance of Feste in** *Twelfth Night*?

INTRODUCTION

Choose three or four arguments to support the title and write a paragraph which sums up your answer to the question. Remember that you will be writing more fully about your chosen arguments in the **body** of your essay. Below are five suggestions:

1. **Explain who Feste is and what he does. This must be included in any essay.**
2. Refer to his independence within the play.
3. **Tell how he does not develop because he has self-knowledge from the beginning. He helps us judge other characters because he has insight into them.**
4. **Explain that he enlightens the characters and the audience** with his wit and songs.
5. **Argue that Feste shows how language can be misused and manipulated.**

INTERNET

Web sites for *Twelfth Night*
The web site for Trevor's Nun's excellent film can be found at:
http://www.flf.com/twelfth/index.html
Background information on jesters can be found at:
http://www.jester.net/

SUGGESTED ESSAY PLAN FOR SHAKESPEARE'S *TWELFTH NIGHT*

For improved expression in your arguments look at the linking words and phrases section on pages 20–21 to help you signpost your argument. Try to link your ideas together and make connections between your points wherever you can.

INTERNET

Web sites for help with Shakespeare plays
Shakespeare Resources:
http://www.sd68.bc.ca/bars/shakespeare.htm
Shakespeare Study Guide with Plot Summaries at:
http://zekscrab.users.50megs.com/Cummings/Shakespeare/index.html

CONCLUSION

- Explain that Feste is a significant character in the play and sum up how he helps our understanding of the play on several levels. This is his dramatic function in the play.
- He is one of the most intelligent characters in the play and yet he has only the status of a fool. His character shows off one of the play's main themes: how a character appears does not necessarily represent their true nature. Appearances can be deceptive!
- Give your views on Feste and say what you have learned through writing this essay.

HOW TO PRODUCE MIND-MAPS FOR ESSAYS

RE-READ YOUR TEXT

Whether you are reading a play, novel or short story, **you must** re-read your text **for a deeper understanding of your** essay question or task. **Many teachers concentrate on scenes from plays and chapters from novels for written assignments.** In plays **they expect pupils to focus on** dramatic technique. **For example, you may be asked to** show how dramatic tension is created in a particular scene. **In** novels **you might be expected to show how a** theme, character, imagery or mood, **has been represented. One of the best ways of making notes for your essay is to produce a** memorable mind-map. **Study your essay question or task and** try to build up relevant comments by looking carefully at key words and phrases in your question.

WHEN TO USE A MIND-MAP

If your essay title asks you to write about a character, theme or any aspect of a text that you are studying you could do a mind-map like the one on the previous spread. Study your essay question and try to build up relevant comments by looking carefully at key words and phrases in your question. Check your ideas again by re-reading key parts of the text.

Examiner's Top Tip
The habit of producing mind-maps or brain-storms that focus on three or four main points will help you plan your answers when you take the final exams.

STUDY THE CHARACTERS

You can learn about characters by examining:

- *what they say*
- *what they do*
- *what other characters say about them*
- *stage directions*
- *how they develop (that is, do they change or do they remain the same? If so, why?)*

BUILD YOUR MIND-MAP AS YOU READ

Go through the play or text and look at the places where your character speaks or others speak about him/her. Build your mind-map up gradually as you do so.

1 Use white paper without lines – it helps you think more clearly.

2 Use a pencil and a rubber – it is quicker and you can add colours, too.

3 Begin in the middle of the page with a title (this could be the name of a character or a theme) and put the most important information around the title.

4 Work your way out to the margins where you should put the least important information.

5 Your first five minutes are likely to be the most productive so do not stop for anything. You can make your map pretty and memorable afterwards.

6 Remember that the colours you choose for various topics of your map can be meaningful because everything can be given an appropriate colour. Colours can also act as prompts to help you recall ideas.

7 You can make connections between ideas by running branches off your main ideas. Draw connecting branches to other main ideas if it seems sensible. Your map will then take on the character of a colourful tube map; you can then add appropriate pictures and images.

8 Remember that pictures will bring ideas to life as well as help you remember them. If you are hopeless at drawing simply cut likely pictures out of magazines.

9 Keep mind-maps to <u>one piece of paper</u>. If you run out of space, tape another sheet of paper on to the side of the paper where you are running out of space. It does not matter how big your piece of paper is as long as it is one side of paper. You can always carefully fold it up afterwards. Boeing, the American aircraft corporation, uses this method to teach their engineers about their aircraft. The corporation has a huge 'quilted' mind-map that takes up the entire length of a hanger! The engineers learn the ins and outs of aircraft design in much less time than conventional methods: months rather than years!

Examiner's Top Tip
Try to get an overview of the themes of your particular play. Then see how a character relates to these themes.

He thinks that Sebastian's use of the word 'vent' is <u>out of place</u>.

Ironically, he is an older, parental figure in a play filled with younger characters.

He shows in his <u>jests</u> to Cesario/Viola how language can be misused.

He thinks of himself not as Olivia's fool but as her 'corrupter of words'.

and he provides <u>comic entertainment</u> and truth-telling through jests and songs.

He is Olivia's 'licensed fool'.

His name suggests the festive element of the play.

He is a wordsmith and is concerned about how language is used.

The main <u>theme</u> of his songs is Carpe Diem ('Seize the day')

The early audiences were lawyers and they played with words too!

Feste's role and function in *Twelfth Night*

Olivia should not mourn and get married.

He helps us understand the other characters.

He has <u>revenge</u> on the proud, puritan, Malvolio who called Feste 'a barren rascal'.

He is uncomfortable with Cesario and hints that he is unreal.

His antagonist, Malvolio is too proud and will commit <u>more folly</u>.

Count Orsino is <u>inconstant</u>.

EXAM QUESTIONS - Use the questions to test your progress. Check your answers on page 94–95.

The Shakespeare Assignment

1. Name two plays you may study.

....

2. Briefly explain a method of understanding passages from Shakespeare.

....

3. Identify two types of assignments that you could produce on a Shakespeare play.

....

4. What does 'textual evidence' mean?

....

5. Can the interpretation of a Shakespeare play change over time?

....

6. If so, why?

....

7. What does 'linguistic devices' mean?

....

8. What are the main genres of Shakespeare plays?

....

9. What does 'philosophical context' mean?

....

10. List the three styles of writing Shakespeare used in his plays.

....

11. Where did he use poetic verse?

....

12. What is the purpose of blank verse?

....

Structure, Themes and How to Produce Mind-maps

13. What does Shakespeare like to establish at the beginning of his plays?

....

14. What happens next?

....

15. What is the 'climax' of a play?

....

16. What could happen during the 'climax' of a play?

....

17. Briefly explain what usually happens at the end of a Shakespeare play.

....

18. What is a 'theme'?

....

19. Identify three themes that can be found in Shakespeare's plays.

....

20. What type of themes might you expect to find in a comedy?

....

21. Briefly explain what is meant by 'dramatic contrast'.

....

22. Why did Shakespeare build dramatic contrasts into his plays?

....

23. Explain what is meant by 'self-knowledge'.

....

24. Briefly sum up the typical structure of a Shakespeare play.

....

Imagery and Essay Plans

25. What is meant by the term 'figures of speech'?

....

26. What is a simile?

....

27. Why is a metaphor a stronger comparison?

....

28. What is an extended metaphor?

....

29. What is meant by personification?

....

30. Define an oxymoron.

....

31. What is a motif?

....

32. Give two reasons why Shakespeare uses imagery in his plays.

....

33. Shakespeare uses a great deal of irony in his plays. What is irony?

....

34. What is dramatic irony?

....

35. Why and where would you expect to find passages rich in imagery?

....

36. Briefly sum up what is meant by imagery.

....

How did you do?

1–9	correct	.start again
10–19	correct	.getting there
20–29	correct	.good work
30–36	correct	.excellent

WHAT YOU HAVE TO STUDY

- <u>Poetry</u> is a significant part of the GCSE language course. This is a little confusing, as most people would rightly think of poetry as <u>literature</u>. However until the criteria for English GCSE changes poetry will account for up to 15% of your final mark.

- Most exam boards test your ability to read and understand poetry in your final exams. Your teacher will select a number of poems, probably by the same poet. The NEAB's poets at present are Simon Armitage, Carol Ann Duffy and Ted Hughes. Other exam boards such as SEG have their own selections of poets or groups of poems under a specific <u>theme</u>.

- The type of poems that you will study will range from <u>ballads</u> (<u>narrative</u> or story poems) to <u>sonnets</u> (serious poems that explore deep themes such as <u>love</u> <u>and</u> <u>death</u>). Some of these poems were written before 1914. With NEAB you will also be expected to study a number of poems under the heading, '<u>Poetry</u> <u>from</u> <u>Other</u> <u>Cultures</u>'. Some exam boards also include prose as an alternative under this or a similar heading. This last section of poetry will be examined on pages 68–71.

Examiner's Top Tip
Do not merely identify figures of speech and other poetic techniques, show how they affect meaning in your poem.

READING A POEM

Aim to read the poems at least <u>three</u> <u>times</u> and do the following very carefully:

- <u>Explain</u> <u>briefly</u> <u>what</u> <u>you</u> <u>think</u> <u>the</u> <u>poem</u> <u>is</u> <u>about.</u> You are looking for <u>an</u> <u>overview</u> at this stage. This early view of the poem may change once you have studied it in greater detail.

- <u>Examine</u> <u>how</u> <u>the</u> <u>poet</u> <u>gets</u> <u>their</u> <u>meaning</u> <u>across</u> <u>to</u> <u>us</u> <u>through</u> <u>their</u> <u>choice</u> <u>of</u> <u>form,</u> <u>language,</u> <u>imagery</u> <u>and</u> <u>themes.</u> You will also need to consider the poem's <u>tone</u>. For instance, what is the <u>attitude</u> of the <u>speaker</u> towards the topic or theme? What is their <u>attitude</u> to you? Does the poem's <u>tone</u> change in the poem? Go through each area as fully as you can.

- <u>Explain</u> <u>your</u> <u>views</u> <u>again</u> <u>on</u> <u>the</u> <u>poem,</u> stating what the poem is about. <u>Point</u> <u>out</u> <u>what</u> <u>can</u> <u>be</u> <u>learned</u> from the poem, including <u>any</u> <u>changes</u> <u>of</u> <u>mind</u> you may have had after working through the first two points given above.

Examiner's Top Tip
Try to write a poem of your own using a specific form. There is a lot to be learned about poetry by trying to write a poem of your own. You may even find that writing poetry gives you pleasure.

Chaucer SHELLEY WORDSWORTH t.s eliot coleridge Keats

HOW YOU WILL BE GRADED

To achieve grades C to A* you will need to:

- show that you have <u>engaged</u> with the poems by giving a <u>sustained</u> and <u>developed</u> <u>response</u> to <u>key words and phrases</u> in your essay question. More sophisticated answers will display <u>an enthusiastic personal response</u> with <u>close textual analysis</u>.

- explore the poems and show <u>insight</u>. Again, more sophisticated responses will show <u>greater insight</u> or <u>exploration</u> of the poems.

- <u>identify</u> the <u>verse form</u> and explain how its <u>genre</u> contributes towards the poem's <u>meaning</u>.

- explain how the poet has used <u>language</u> and <u>imagery</u> in the poem. In other words you will need to be able to identify word choices (<u>diction</u>) and what they may suggest as well as show how the poet uses <u>figures of speech</u>, such as <u>similes</u>, to <u>add meaning</u> to their <u>ideas</u> and <u>messages</u> in their poems. More developed responses will <u>show how the poet uses</u> similar <u>themes or points and ideas in several poems</u>. Such responses will also point out <u>similarities</u> or <u>contrasts</u> in the poet's use of <u>language, form</u> and other aspects of <u>poetic technique</u>.

- say something about the poet's <u>purposes</u> and <u>intentions</u>. What is the poet setting out to achieve?

- identify with the <u>poet's intentions</u> or the <u>view of the narrator</u> in the poem. In other words show <u>empathy</u>.

- give a sophisticated response that is <u>convincing</u> and <u>imaginative, showing a high degree of empathy</u>.

- display <u>analytical</u> and <u>interpretive</u> skills when examining the <u>social, moral</u> and <u>philosophical significance</u> of the poems.

HOW TO STUDY AND WRITE ABOUT POETRY (EN2)

QUICK TEST

1. How much of your final mark is your work on poetry likely to be worth?
2. What kind of poem is a ballad?
3. Where would you write your personal views in an exam essay?
4. How many times should you read a poem?
5. What is empathy?

5. Identifying with the theme or idea in a poem or perhaps the narrator's point of view.
4. At least three times.
3. At the end of your essay.
2. A narrative poem.
1. 15%

WRITING ABOUT POETRY (EN2)

TIPS ON WRITING ABOUT POETRY

One of the biggest problems in writing about poetry is finding <u>phrases</u> that enable you to <u>express</u> your <u>ideas</u> and make your writing <u>flow</u>. This <u>framework</u> is not really meant as a substitute for your structure, just a helping hand in case you get stuck. You should aim <u>to integrate useful phrases into your writing</u> so that you can explain yourself with ease in exams. Beware, however, of always using the same phrases, which would lead to a <u>mechanical style</u>.

- Introduce points that you want to make by using some of the phrases given below; change them around, or simply add them together. The more <u>fluent</u> you are the more <u>impressive</u> your points will be.

- Good grades in exams are achieved through <u>knowing your texts</u> and being able to <u>express</u> your points in a <u>fluent manner</u>. You will also be judged on your <u>punctuation</u>, your use of <u>standard English</u> and the <u>quality</u> <u>of your expression</u>.

- Look out for useful ways of <u>expressing</u> your <u>ideas</u> and making a note of them. Successful pupils are able to make their points in essays in a <u>fluent</u> and knowledgeable manner.

Examiner's Top Tip
Remember P.E.C. Point: make a point to address your question. Evidence: give a word, phrase or line of evidence for it. Comment: comment on your evidence and link it to the question.

1. INTRODUCTORY PHRASES

- **The poem . . . is/seems to be about . . .**
- **The poem is narrated in the <u>first/second</u> <u>person</u>. This aids/enhances the poem's meaning as/because . . .**
- **The form of the poem is (a <u>ballad</u>/<u>sonnet</u>/<u>two-</u>, <u>three-</u>, <u>four-</u>, <u>five-line</u> <u>stanzas</u>/<u>free verse</u>) . . . This is an <u>appropriate</u> form for the poem because it helps readers <u>appreciate</u> . . .**

2. PHRASES FOR THE MIDDLE OF A PIECE OF WRITING

- The theme/idea of . . . is present/repeated in both poems.
- For instance . . . . The poet contrasts . . . with . . . .
- The poet uses appropriate language/diction to convey a feeling of . . . . For instance . . .
- The caesura after . . . helps an audience understand . . . .
- The use of alliteration/assonance/onomatopoeia with . . . shows . . . .
- The poet's use of imagery (similes/metaphors/personification) can be seen with . . . . This shows/ intensifies the idea of . . . .
- Another interesting example of this is . . . . . This emphasises/shows/reinforces/gives a sense of/ refers to . . . .
- The poem's meaning is enhanced /deepened with . . .
- An example of which is . . . . This refers to the main idea of . . . .
- For example, this can be seen with . . . .
- The poem reflects the narrator's/poet's feelings on/of . . . .
- The poet reminds the reader of . . . with . . . .
- The poet draws attention to the fact that . . . .
- The poet compares . . . with . . . .

Examiner's Top Tip

It is important to be precise when writing about poetry. Remember that 'verse' means the whole poem or a collection of poems. You should use 'stanza' when you want to describe a part of a poem, such as a four-line 'quatrain'.

3. PHRASES TO SUM UP YOUR ARGUMENTS AND VIEWS

- *The poem's/narrator's tone is one of . . . . This helps the reader/audience appreciate the/how . . .*
- *The tone(s) in each poem is/are . . . . This/these show(s) . . .*
- *To sum up I would say that the poet feels . . . about his/her subject. The poet wants us to understand/feel the . . .*
- *Both/each of the poems show . . . . This shows the poet's feelings of . . .*
- *From reading these poems I learned that . . .*
- *My final view of the poem (s) is that it is /they are . . .*

QUICK TEST

1. What does P.E.C. mean?
2. Find out what the term 'caesura' means.
3. Find out the number of lines in a sonnet.
4. What is alliteration?
5. What is a writing frame?

COMPARING TWO OR MORE POEMS

FROM THE ENGLISH LITERARY HERITAGE (EN2)

ESSAY QUESTION

In an exam, the first thing that you need to do is work out which poems are most suitable to write about given the key words and phrases in the question. Of course, if the examiner identifies the poems that you must write about and gives you bullet points to help you, then your essay plan has been written for you.

Explain how outsiders are portrayed in *War Photographer* and *Stealing* by Carol Ann Duffy

WRITE ABOUT:
- how the photographer and the thief are portrayed
- what is suggested by the imagery associated with them
- your view of the poems

Finish off by briefly giving your personal views on the poems and relate them to the essay question.

WHAT THE POEMS ARE ABOUT

- Both poems are about <u>outsiders</u> of society who have unusual occupations. One is a war photographer and the other a thief. Both poems explore their work. The two characters share highly developed visual skills.
- The poems explore the <u>motives</u> of these outsiders: the photographer sees his work as a duty to those who die even if his audience ultimately 'do not care'. The thief tries to explain his or her reasons for theft; however the theft of the snowman seems pointless and it is carried out because he or she is alone and bored. Both thief and photographer feel that they are misunderstood by society.

HOW EACH POEM'S MEANING IS EXPRESSED

- The <u>point</u> <u>of</u> <u>view</u> is different for each poem. War Photographer is narrated by a respectful, third-person narrator. Stealing is narrated in the <u>first</u> <u>person</u>; the style is that of a dramatic monologue in which the thief is the sole speaker in the poem. Its speaker is a streetwise, defensive thief who talks in an abrupt manner as if he or she answering questions in an interview.
- In Stealing the age and sex of the thief are not given, and although we are told that the war photographer is a man it seems there is a sense of anonymity in both poems. This <u>sense</u> of <u>ambiguity</u> reinforces the sense of each being an outsider.
- The four regular stanzas of War Photographer stress the <u>repetitive</u> and <u>cyclical</u> <u>nature</u> of the photographer's work as he comes and goes between jobs. The form of Stealing is five, five-line stanzas of irregular length with several run-on lines with a start-stop feel. The five stanzas and its style of first-person narration are in keeping with the lack of harmony of its narrator and the thief's terse and self-justifying <u>dramatic</u> <u>monologue</u>.
- The <u>imagery</u> in each poem is focused on the activities, feelings and motives of each character. The thief, for example, feels 'alone' and steals the snowman because he or she wants 'a mate' who is as cold-hearted as him or her. The thief suffers from low self-esteem. The thief thinks of him or herself as a film star. This is evident as the thief watches his or her 'gloved hand twisting the doorknob' of 'A stranger's bedroom'. Many of the items stolen represent the thief's aspirations for a more successful, glamorous life.
- As the photographer develops the pictures in his 'dark room' he is compared with a priest. The imagery helps readers appreciate his sense of duty to the dead as he anxiously develops his film. In the process the suffering that he witnessed is vividly recalled by Duffy's <u>ambiguous</u> <u>use</u> <u>of</u> <u>language</u>. This can be seen with 'the half-formed ghost' of a dying man that appears before the photographer's eyes.
- Duffy deliberately uses the present tense in each poem. This gives the poems a sense of <u>immediacy</u> that enhances their impact. It creates a tone of <u>tension</u> and later <u>irony</u> in War Photographer. In Stealing the <u>present</u> <u>tense</u> enhances the clipped prose of the thief; it is as if he or she is giving an interview and being, albeit momentarily and pathetically, a star.

MAKING REVISION NOTES

This is an example of how to make revision notes on Duffy's remaining poems. Although we are studying *Stealing* and *War Photographer,* the themes and images can be applied to some of Duffy's other poems. The themes here are related to the *War Photographer* and can be found in most of Carol Ann Duffy's Poems in the *Neab Anthology:*

DIFFERENT KINDS OF LOVE

War Photographer is not as strongly linked to the theme of Different Kinds of Love. However, it could be argued that the third-person narrator in War Photographer approaches love in his admiration and respect for the dedicated photographer. The photographer, who is compared with a priest, bravely gets his pictures; he only becomes nervous in the relative safety of England as he fears that one slip could spoil the photographs and thus prevent his evidence of the suffering of war victims becoming known. It is as if he is 'a priest' carrying out a sacred rite; he acts as a witness for those who suffered. Perhaps the photographer sees his actions not just as his duty but as an act of love and humanity.

MEMORIES OF THE PAST

The photographer develops photos of a recent assignment in which a man died in a country at war. The poem is narrated in the present tense. This makes the photographer's ritualistic, priest-like actions seem more vivid and sacred as he nervously develops his pictures. It is as if he is undertaking a duty to the dead. He is our witness.

OUTSIDERS

The photographer does an unusual job because he works in war-torn countries and then returns to the comparative safety of England. He works alone and he needs to have excellent visual skills. He acts as a witness, 'priest' and go-between. The poem shows what his life is like. But do we, the public, care that deeply about what he brings back and develops for us?

OTHER PEOPLE'S LIVES

- The poem deals with the life of the photographer. It also reveals who suffers, including close relatives. The photographer's editor is also unveiled as someone only interested in looking to 'pick five or six' striking photos for the free parts of a newspaper. The public reacts sympathetically to the pictures in 'Sunday's supplement' but they soon forget the impact of the photographs as they get on with their consumer-led lives. The narrator's ironic internal rhyme towards the end of the poem shows contempt for the readers who cannot feel anything for very long, and an enduring sympathy for the photographer.

- Internal rhyme often introduces a comic tone in poetry. It occurs in pairs of words within lines and not in line endings.

- The third person's tone in War Photographer is serious and respectful towards the photographer; however the tone changes when the narrator considers the short-lived concerns of readers. News is a 24-hour commodity in the western world where fresh news stories quickly erase the impact of stories only a few hours before. The words 'tears' and 'beers' add a touch of bathos as they undercut the previous serious mood in the poem and therefore serve as an ironic comment by the narrator on the consumers who buy newspapers. They quickly forget any feelings they may have had within a few hours over an afternoon drink:
'...The reader's eyeballs prick
With tears between the bath and pre-lunch beers.'

- This notion of the emotional shallowness of modern society, as well as the cynical nature of the photographer's job, is reinforced by the final lines of the poem, as the photographer flies out on another assignment:
'From the aeroplane he stares impassively at where he earns his living and they do not care.'

This is an example of how you could make revision notes on Duffy's remaining poems. Try to look for ideas that seem to be repeated in the poems that you are studying. These themes can be found in most of Carol Ann Duffy's Poems in the NEAB Anthology. Choose a theme and find evidence in the poems for these links. Make notes like those above or in the form of chart if you prefer.

Linking Theme	Different Kinds of Love	Memories of the Past	Outsiders	Other People's Lives
War Photographer	✓	✓	✓	✓
Stealing		✓	✓	✓
Valentine	✓			
Before You Were Mine	✓	✓	✓	✓
Mrs Tilcher's Class	✓	✓		

TEXTS FROM OTHER CULTURES AND TRADITIONS (EN2)

English from around the world

WHAT YOU MAY STUDY

You will either study a number of <u>poems</u>, or <u>short</u> <u>stories</u> or <u>novels</u> written by English speakers from different countries around the world. Whether you write about these texts for coursework or for your final exams depends upon the <u>syllabus</u> of the exam board that your school is following. Whatever you study you will need to adopt the same approach. In your course-work or exam answers you will need to:

- show that you <u>understand</u> what you have read and <u>know</u> <u>how</u> <u>it</u> <u>relates</u> to other texts in 'Other Cultures and Traditions'.

- display an <u>awareness</u> of the <u>themes</u> <u>and</u> <u>ideas</u> in the texts which make them <u>distinctive</u>.

- make <u>comparisons</u> between the texts in your essays.

FINDING LINKS BETWEEN THE POEMS

Look for <u>common</u> <u>ideas</u> or <u>themes</u> that can help you make <u>links</u> between the stories or poems you study. Among such <u>ideas</u> and <u>themes</u> try to find:

ideas about <u>language</u>, <u>power</u> and <u>dialect</u>

feelings about being <u>caught</u> <u>between</u> two <u>cultures</u>

feelings about <u>change</u> <u>or</u> <u>how</u> <u>things</u> <u>do</u> <u>not</u> <u>change</u>

ideas about <u>language</u> <u>and</u> <u>identity</u>

<u>beliefs</u> <u>and</u> <u>ritual</u>

<u>protest</u> <u>against</u> <u>ideas</u> <u>and</u> <u>attitudes</u> (this will include <u>racism</u>)

feelings about <u>independence</u>

differences in <u>attitudes</u> <u>and</u> <u>values</u>

<u>customs</u> <u>and</u> <u>traditions</u>

HOW YOU WILL BE GRADED

To achieve grades C to A* or higher you will need to <u>compare</u> the texts. As you do so you should:

- show an <u>understanding</u> of the texts' <u>main</u> <u>characters</u>.
- give a <u>sustained</u> and <u>developed</u> knowledge of the texts and show an <u>awareness</u> of the writers' <u>purposes</u>.
- show <u>insight</u> and the <u>ability</u> to <u>explore</u> these texts.
- reveal <u>a</u> <u>structured</u> <u>understanding</u> of how <u>thoughts</u> <u>and</u> <u>feelings</u> are revealed in the texts.
- <u>display</u> <u>an</u> <u>awareness</u> of how <u>form</u>, <u>language</u> and <u>imagery</u> are used and <u>comment</u> on how these contribute towards <u>meaning</u> in the texts.
- make <u>effective</u> <u>use</u> of <u>textual</u> <u>detail</u> to <u>support</u> <u>your</u> <u>arguments</u>. At higher levels reveal <u>a</u> <u>convincing</u> and <u>imaginative</u> <u>interpretation</u> of the texts.
- show involvement through <u>personal</u> <u>empathy</u>. That is, <u>appreciate</u> the writer's <u>concerns</u>, <u>ideas</u> or <u>attitudes</u>. At the higher levels you will exhibit <u>a</u> <u>high</u> <u>degree</u> <u>of</u> <u>empathy</u>.
- place people and powerful <u>emotions</u> in the context of <u>local</u> <u>customs</u> and <u>traditions</u>.
- engage with texts by showing <u>an</u> <u>enthusiastic</u> <u>personal</u> <u>response</u>. But be honest – you do not have to

SOME ESSENTIAL POETIC TERMS

USE OF LETTER AND WORD SOUNDS

- Alliteration: the same consonant at the beginning of words repeated for an effect: 'fireside flickers'.
- Assonance: repetition of vowel sounds for an effect: 'icy winds knife us'. The repetition of the vowel 'i' helps stress the coldness of the 'winds'.
- Onomatopoeia: words which sound like their meaning: 'buzz' and 'click'.
- Rhythm and rhyme: the poem's pace when read aloud and word endings that sound alike for an effect.

IMAGERY

- Metaphor: a stronger comparison where 'is' or 'are' is used or implied: 'Juliet is the sun.'
- Personification: ('person-making'): giving an animal, idea or noun human feelings to enhance an emotion, feeling or effect: 'Arise fair sun and kill the envious moon.'
- Oxymoron: Figures of speech in which contradictory, opposite words are yoked together for an effect. For example, The Beatles, the great 1960s pop band, famously had a hit song and a film entitled A Hard Day's Night.
  Oxymorons can also be paradoxes to enliven prose but some have turned into clichés: 'act naturally', 'living dead', etc.
- Simile: a comparison using 'as' or 'like': 'My love is as deep as the sea.'

PUNCTUATION AND FORM

- Ballad: a story poem that usually features dramatic stories about ordinary people.
- Couplet: a two-line stanza that rhymes.
- Caesura or Cesura: means 'a cutting'. It can be any type of punctuation in poetry that causes the reader to pause. Poets use them to end-stop their lines and to emphasise points and ideas in their poetry. A caesura can add a great deal of meaning if placed in the middle of a line.
- Elegy: a poem for a dead person.

- Enjambment or run-on line/run-on stanza: one line runs into another to achieve a poetic effect, often used to aid rhythm and help enact something.
- Free verse: irregular stanzas, filled with lines of varying length. The lines are like waves coming in along a sea-shore: each has natural rhythm and is just long enough. The form suits conversational and argumentative poems. Free verse, or vers libre, was the most popular form of poetry in the twentieth century and still remains so.
- Lyric: a poem that sets out the thoughts and feelings of a single speaker.
- Quatrain: four lines of a poem that rhyme. It is the main unit in English poetry.
- Stanza: a clear section of a poem, usually two or four lines.
- Sonnet: usually a 14-line poem about a serious theme such as love or death.
- Triplet or Tercet: a three-line stanza; this is a form suited for comic poetry, but watch out for when poets reverse the expected content, as with Seamus Heaney's Mid-Term Break. The effect can be very poignant.
- Verse: an entire poem or collection of poems or poetry.

NARRATIVE STANCE AND ATTITUDES WITHIN POEMS

- Narrator (first and third person): if the whole poem is spoken by the first-person narrator then this is known as a dramatic monologue. For an example, read Robert Browning's poem My Last Duchess.
- Tone: a poet's or narrator's attitude towards their subject and audience. Note that tone can change within a poem to emphasise changes of meaning. The poet's use of diction (words deliberately chosen for their associations and sounds) can affect the tone of a poem. For example, one-syllable words can create a soft, spell-like effect. Carol Ann Duffy uses several words that have religious associations in the first stanza of War Photographer to create a hushed, respectful tone for the photographer as he develops his photographs in his 'dark room'.

QUICK TEST

1. What is a simile?
2. Explain what empathy means.
3. Give an example of onomatopoeia.
4. What is the difference between 'verse' and a 'stanza'?
5. What is a suitable subject for a sonnet and why?

1. A comparison using 'as' or 'like'.
2. An appreciation of a writer's or narrator's concerns and ideas.
3. Buzz (or any word that sounds like its meaning)
4. 'Verse' is an entire poem or collection of poems; a 'stanza' is a section of a poem
5. 'Love' or 'death' because sonnets usually have serious subject matter.

Examiner's Top Tip
It is not enough simply to identify poetic terms – you have got to show how they add meaning to a poem.

Half-Caste

5.

Excuse me
standing on one leg
I'm half-caste

Explain yuself
what yu mean
when yu say half-caste
yu mean when picasso
mix red an green
is a half-caste canvas
explain yuself
wha yu mean
when yu say half-caste
yu mean when light an shadow
mix in de sky
is a half-caste weather
well in dat case
england weather
nearly always half-caste
in fact some o dem cloud
half-caste till dem overcast
so spiteful dem dont want de sun pass
ah rass
explain yuself
wha yu mean
when yu say half-caste
yu mean tchaikovsky
sit down at dah piano
an mix a black key
wid a white key
is a half-caste symphony

Explain yuself
wha yu mean
Ah listening to yu wid de keen
half of mih ear
Ah lookin at yu wid de keen
half of mih eye
and when I'm introduced to yu

I'm sure you'll understand
why I offer yu half-a-hand
an when I sleep at night
I close half-a-eye
consequently when I dream
I dream half-a-dream
an when moon begin to glow
I half-caste human being
cast half-a-shadow
but yu must come back tomorrow
wid de whole of yu eye
an de whole of yu ear
an de whole of yu mind

6.

an I will tell yu
de other half
of my story

John Agard

Unrelated Incidents

1.

2.

this is thi
six a clock
news thi
man said n
thi reason
a talk wia
BBC accent
iz coz yi
widny wahnt
mi ti talk
aboot thi
trooth wia
voice lik
wanna yoo
scruff. if
a toktaboot
thi trooth
lik wanna yoo
scruff yi
widny thingk
it wuz troo.
jist wonna yoo
scruff tokn.
thirza right
way ti spell
ana right way
ti tok it. this
is me tokn yir
right way a
spellin. this
is ma trooth.
yooz doant no
thi trooth
yirsellz cawz
yi canny talk
right. this is
the six a clock
nyooz. belt up.

3.

4.

Tom Leonard

Important Point

In an exam you will be unlikely to write as much as this. You will also need to give more brief quotations to support your points than are given above. Even so, a few points made well with appropriately chosen evidence would secure you a good mark.

INTERNET

Useful exercises and ideas about 'Poems And Texts from Other Cultures' and help with other exam poetry and texts can be found at:
www.englishresources.co.uk

WHAT THE POEMS ARE ABOUT

1. Both poems deal with issues of <u>language</u>, <u>power</u> and <u>prejudice</u>.

2. Leonard <u>ironically</u> reverses the usual <u>dialects</u> associated with <u>authority</u> and reading the news (<u>received pronunciation</u> and <u>standard</u> <u>English</u>). He wants us to think about issues of <u>truth</u> and <u>authority</u> when we only hear the news read by people with <u>received</u> <u>pronunciation</u> or <u>standard</u> <u>English</u>.

3. He argues that it is wrong and prejudiced to believe that these <u>dialects</u> are the only ones capable of expressing the truth and so be taken seriously. His angry <u>narrator</u> shows that such prejudice is silly and wrong, especially as <u>the</u> <u>narrator</u> <u>argues</u> <u>that</u> <u>his</u> working-class Glaswegian dialect <u>is</u> <u>the</u> <u>only</u> <u>one</u> <u>which</u> <u>should</u> <u>taken</u> <u>seriously;</u> it is as if the local dialect is a cut above anyone else's because it is the only one capable of expressing the 'trooth'. Leonard infers that <u>'trooth'</u> <u>can</u> <u>be</u> <u>told</u> <u>in</u> <u>any</u> <u>dialect</u>.

4. The <u>tone</u> of his poem <u>is</u> <u>one</u> <u>of</u> <u>anger</u> <u>against</u> <u>the</u> <u>prejudices</u> <u>of</u> <u>society</u> where working-class dialects are not taken seriously and given no respect. Leonard thinks that speakers of <u>local</u> <u>dialects</u> are not given the consideration and status that they deserve.

5. Agard's <u>narrator</u> eloquently shows, through a number of unusual and convincing <u>comparisons,</u> that it is wrong to label anyone by using the term 'half-caste'. The unquestioned use of such terms can lead to the prejudice of seeing someone as only <u>half</u> <u>a</u> <u>person</u>.

6. Agard and Leonard show us that <u>power,</u> <u>authority</u> <u>and</u> <u>prejudice</u> <u>are</u> <u>linked</u> <u>with</u> <u>language</u> <u>and</u> <u>how</u> <u>we</u> <u>use</u> <u>it</u>. They warn us against blindly accepting some dialects, such as standard <u>English</u>, as voices of <u>authority</u> and <u>correctness</u> while excluding others and their speakers as only worthy of ridicule. <u>The</u> <u>'truth'</u> <u>can</u> <u>be</u> <u>expressed</u> <u>in</u> <u>other</u> <u>dialects</u> <u>too</u>.

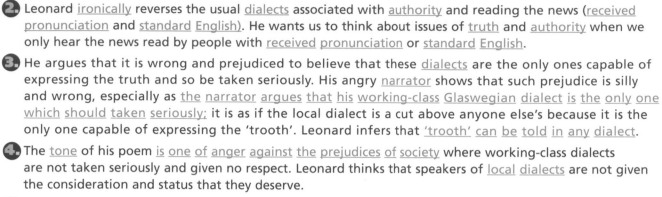

HOW TO COMPARE TEXTS FROM OTHER CULTURES (EN2)

You have to write a comparative essay comparing two or more texts. On these pages there are examples of what you should try to achieve. Your first aim in exams is to write about poems that are naturally linked through themes, ideas, or layout. See the previous pages for suggestions on linking the poems or texts.
• Write about the importance of language and form in *Half-Caste*
(by John Agard) and *Unrelated Incidents* (by Tom Leonard).

HOW MEANING IN THE POEMS IS EXPRESSED

• **The impact of each poem's argument is enhanced through being spoken by a <u>first-person</u> <u>narrator</u>. Both are appropriately set out in <u>free</u> <u>verse</u>, in which the dialect is defiantly proclaimed and <u>phonetically</u> spelled in <u>lines</u> <u>of</u> <u>varying</u> <u>length</u>. The narrowness of the poems' lines contrast with other poems written in <u>standard</u> <u>English</u>. The poets may intend the form of their poems to act as a badge for the dignity, independence and truthfulness of their dialects. The form of each poem is thus appropriate for the arguments and language deployed by the poets.**

• **The rules of <u>standard</u> <u>English</u> have no place in these poems as there is no punctuation, nor capital letters. The <u>narrators</u> make their points with <u>questions,</u> <u>arguments</u> <u>and</u> <u>statements</u>. The idea is to advance <u>an</u> <u>alternative</u> <u>to</u> <u>standard</u> <u>English.</u> Agard's poem has <u>stanzas</u> in which some of the <u>senses</u> are alluded to. Leonard's poem is plainer, using a single stanza or <u>verse</u> <u>paragraph</u> to refer to speech and <u>Glaswegian</u> <u>dialect</u>. The poets may be from different parts of the world yet there is a similarity in their views on language about <u>what</u> should be said and <u>how</u> it should be expressed.**

• **Both poems have <u>an</u> <u>ironic</u> <u>tone</u> intended to startle their audiences into accepting the truth of the arguments that they advance. Phrases such as 'belt up' and 'ah rass' disclose their respective <u>tones</u>.**

Examiner's Top Tip
You only have half an hour in your exam. Make a few points well. Give evidence for each point and comment on it. You cannot say everything!

Try to tie the main comparative points of the poems together briefly and give your views.

EXAM QUESTIONS - Use the questions to test your progress. Check your answers on page 95.

How to Read and Study Poetry

1. How much of your final mark is represented by both sections of poetry in your exam?

....

2. Are you being tested on your reading or your writing?

....

3. Name two forms for poems.

....

4. How many times should you read your poems?

....

5. What is tone?

....

6. What are the main forms of narration?

....

7. Diction is another word for the word choices that poets make for their poems. True or false?

....

8. What is a theme?

....

9. Part of a poem is a verse. True or false?

....

10. You only need to write about one poem. True or false?

....

11. The classroom 'glowed like a sweet shop' is a metaphor. True or false?

....

12. Briefly explain the three stages of reading and understanding poetry.

....

How to Write About Poems

13. How many poems do you need to compare in your final exam?

....

14. What is enjambment?

....

15. What does it mean to 'compare and contrast' when writing about poetry?

....

16. What is an oxymoron?

....

17. What can an oxymoron suggest?

....

18. Quatrains are the main units of English poetry. True or false?

....

19. What is free verse?

....

20. Why is free verse appropriate for certain poems?

....

21. What is assonance?

....

22. Why do poets use caesuras?

....

23. Where should you give your personal view of the poems that you write about?

....

24. If you cannot write about everything that you would like to, what is the best way to get a good grade?

....

Texts from Other Cultures and Traditions

25. What are 'Texts from Other Cultures and Traditions'?

....

26. What form is most favoured by poets from 'Other Cultures and Traditions'?

....

27. Identify two dialects spoken by poets from other cultures.

....

28. Name three texts by writers or poets of 'Other Cultures or Traditions' from the exam syllabus that you are following.

....

29. Give three themes or ideas that can be explored these texts.

....

30. Once you identify a figure of speech or some other poetic technique what must you do afterwards?

....

31. John Agard uses no caesuras in his poem. True or false?

....

32. The narrow lines of Tom Leonard and John Agard's poems suit the dialect that they use. True or false?

....

33. Why do Tom Leonard and John Agard use free verse?

....

34. In his poem Half-Caste John Agard argues that the unthinking use of the standard English phrase 'half-caste' leads to negative implications. What are these implications?

....

35. How long do you have to plan and write your essay in the final exam?

....

36. Identify two poems from 'Other Cultures' in the NEAB Anthology that are connected by the theme of change. If you are studying with another exam board identify a theme that is present in two or more texts.

....

How did you do?

1–9	correct	.....start again
10–19	correct	.....getting there
20–29	correct	.....good work
30–36	correct	.....excellent

WHAT YOU WILL STUDY

You will be given **a theme** **or** **an issue** and asked to **explore** **it** **in** **two** **texts**. The text written before 1914 must be in **prose**. You may be asked to make a **comparison** of the texts; that is, draw attention to any **similarities**. Conversely, you may be asked to make a **contrast** between the texts; that means **explain** **what** **is** **different** about them.

You can compare:
• **novels**
• **plays**
• **stories**
• **poems**
• **or any combination of the above as long as the first text is written in prose and was written before 1914 and the second text was written by an author of literary merit.**

To **achieve** **the** **higher** **grades** you will need to **include** some discussion of the **social, historical** **or** **cultural** **setting** of your chosen texts.

Examiner's Top Tip
The term 'text' can refer to any form of writing and you should refer to your books, stories or poems as texts in your writing.

Points to Remember

• You need to compare two texts.
• The texts can be from different genres.
• One text must be in prose and written before 1914 by an author recognised within the National Curriculum.
• To get a high grade you will need to include some historical, literary, or cultural context.
• Aim to create skilful transitions between your points in your paragraphs. Write a sentence or so to introduce your points or tie your arguments together.

HOW YOU WILL BE GRADED

You will be assessed on your **ability** **to** **read** **and** **show** **your** **understanding** **through writing on your chosen** **texts**.

To achieve grades C to A* you should aim to **show** **insight**:
• by making relevant points on the **similarities** and **differences** between texts and by noting the implications of what is the same and what is different.
• by making **relevant** points **and** **arguments** on **characters** and the **style** in which the **texts** are written.
• by showing **an** **awareness** of how your texts are **structured,** **making** **relevant.** **comparative** **points** where you can.

To get a grade A or better you will need to **show** **analytical** **skills** as you **explore**:
• the **relevance** of the **historical** **context** or **background** of **texts.**
• how the **text's** **language** is **characteristic** of the writer and his or her **time.**
• the **themes,** **ideas** **and** **irony** **of** **the** **texts.** You should try to **show** **originality** **in** **your** **analysis.**
• the **writer's** **craft**: how writers create their **effects** and how they appeal to their **audiences** through the use of **figurative** or **emotive** **language** for implication or suggestion.
• the **significance** of the writer's **achievements** within the **prose-fiction** **genre.**
• the **moral** and **philosophical** **context** and significance of the **texts.**

POSSIBLE ASSIGNMENTS

Remember that you need to do some <u>research</u> on the <u>background</u> of your <u>texts</u>. This is because you will need to show an awareness of the <u>social</u>, <u>historical</u> <u>and</u> <u>cultural</u> <u>background</u> for each <u>text</u> in your essay.

You could write an essay about:

- <u>social</u> <u>relationships</u> between women and men.
- the <u>presentation</u> of women.
- <u>change</u> through <u>education</u> and <u>experience</u>.
- the <u>theme</u> <u>of</u> <u>change</u> from <u>innocence</u> <u>to</u> <u>experience</u>.
- <u>the</u> <u>effects</u> <u>of</u> <u>technological</u> <u>change</u>.
- how<u> relationships between two generations</u> are <u>presented</u>.
- the <u>presentation</u> of <u>outsiders</u> in literature.
- <u>ambition</u> <u>and</u> <u>jealousy</u>.
- the <u>theme</u> of <u>good</u> and <u>evil</u>.
- the use of <u>myth</u> in literature.
- <u>appearance</u> <u>and</u> <u>reality</u> leading to <u>self-knowledge</u>.
- the <u>country</u> <u>and</u> <u>the</u> <u>city</u> and the values and problems associated with each of them.
- <u>two</u> <u>detectives</u> <u>from</u> <u>different</u> <u>eras</u>. You could compare and contrast the working relationship of Sir Arthur Conan Doyle's Sherlock Holmes and Dr Watson with Colin Dexter's Inspector Morse and Sergeant Lewis.
- <u>stories</u> <u>with</u> <u>similar</u> <u>themes</u> or ideas such as 'growing up' or 'change'.
- <u>Compare</u> <u>and</u> <u>contrast</u> any pre-1914 story by a recognised author in the National Curriculum with a story from the NEAB Anthology or any other collection of stories issued by the exam boards. Most teachers have a few favoured stories that they use for comparative assignments. The main thing here is that the modern text has literary merit and is worthy of study.

STUDYING NOVELS AND SHORT STORIES (EN2)

QUICK TEST

1. Identify two types of texts that you will be asked to compare.

2. What are the two important rules about the older texts?

3. What is the context of a text?

4. What can a 'text' be?

5. You will be assessed on your reading skills. True or false?

1. The first text before 1914 must be by an author of literary merit.
2. The texts must have been written before 1914 and by an author named in the National Curriculum.
3. The time and the events which took place when it was written.
4. Any written piece of work.
5. True, but you will also need good written skills to show you've understood what you've read.

LITERARY TECHNIQUE: NARRATORS, CHARACTERISATION AND DIALOGUE (EN2)

WHAT TO LOOK FOR IN CHARACTERS

When you are studying the <u>characters</u> in your novel, you should look out for the following things:

- The <u>names</u> of <u>characters</u> sometimes tell you more about them. For example, Pip from *Great Expectations* is named after a seed. One of the novel's main <u>themes</u> is his development and growth as he changes from a lower-class boy to a gentleman. The novel charts the education of his heart as well as his mind.

- What <u>characters</u> <u>look</u> <u>like</u>. The <u>physical</u> <u>appearance</u> of characters given in their <u>description</u> often tells us more about them.

- What a character <u>says</u> <u>and</u> <u>does</u>. Much can be inferred from <u>talk</u> and <u>action</u>.

- <u>Flat</u> and <u>round</u> <u>characters</u>. E.M. Forster created these terms to describe types of characters found in novels in his book *Aspects of the Novel* (1927). <u>Flat</u> <u>characters</u> <u>do</u> <u>not</u> <u>develop</u> in novels and are generally <u>not</u> <u>as</u> <u>important</u> <u>as</u> <u>round</u> <u>characters</u>, <u>who</u> <u>develop</u> because they change in the course of a novel. The same terms can be applied to characters in short stories.

- How a character <u>interacts</u> with other characters.

- What <u>other</u> <u>characters</u> say about him or her. This can help readers understand other aspects of a character's <u>personality</u>.

- Any <u>direct</u> <u>comments</u> on the character by a <u>third-person</u> <u>narrator</u>.

- If the <u>character</u> that you are studying is the <u>narrator</u> of your story, how far can you trust what he or she says? Do they have <u>self-knowledge</u> or do they have a lot to learn? Could they be termed an <u>unreliable</u> <u>narrator</u>?

Examiner's Top Tip
Always check to see if a story is written in the first or third person.

FIRST- OR THIRD-PERSON NARRATOR?

- Notice <u>how</u> writers tell their stories. Do they tell the story from the <u>point</u> <u>of</u> <u>view</u> of a character <u>within</u> the story as '<u>I</u>' or '<u>me</u>' – that is, as a <u>first-person</u> narrator? Or have they chosen to write about the story from the <u>point</u> <u>of</u> <u>view</u> of someone who looks at what is going on from <u>outside</u> the story and in which the narrator says '<u>he</u>', '<u>she</u>' or '<u>they</u>'? The writer's choice of <u>who</u> <u>tells</u> <u>the</u> <u>story</u> <u>can</u> <u>determine</u> <u>how</u> <u>we</u> <u>see, understand</u> <u>and</u> <u>interpret</u> <u>characters, as</u> <u>well</u> <u>as</u> <u>themes</u> <u>and</u> <u>ideas</u> within a story.

- <u>First-person</u> narrators usually have a <u>limited</u> point <u>of</u> <u>view</u>. They are so close to what is happening that they cannot see everything that is going on or know what other characters are thinking.

- <u>Third-person</u> narrators can see and know much more. They can know everything if the writer wants them to. This last kind of narrator is called <u>an</u> <u>omniscient</u> narrator.

- It is important to understand that whatever the <u>first-</u> <u>or</u> <u>third-person</u> <u>narrator</u> thinks is not necessarily what the <u>writer</u> thinks. Show in your writing that you understand that <u>writers</u> <u>adopt</u> <u>masks</u> <u>by</u> <u>using</u> <u>narrators</u> in their stories.

DIALOGUE

- **Dialogue is speech between two or more characters.** In novels this is more than mere communication; it makes **characters seem more vivid** and **lifelike**.

- Dialogue helps readers **learn** about characters; they reveal their **aims, motives, personalities** and **outlooks** through what they say and the words and phrases that they use.

- **Dialogue shows what characters think about other characters.** This also helps **us** make up our minds about them and understand how they relate to the main **themes, messages** and **ideas** in a story.

An example of **third-person** narration and **characterisation** from Penelope Lively's short story, *The Darkness Out There*:

- Innocent, young Sandra reassures herself with daydreams of a better life as she walks through the dark, creepy wood of Packer's End to do her good deed of housework for old Mrs Rutter:
'She put her sandal back on. She walked through the thicker grass by the hedge and felt it drag at her legs and thought of swimming in warm seas. She put her hand on the top of her head and her hair was hot from the sun, a dry burning cap. One day, this year, next year, sometime, she would go to places like on travel brochures and run into a blue sea. She would fall in love and she would get a good job and she would have one of those new Singers that do zig-zag stitch and make an embroidered silk coat.'

An example of **first-person** **narration** and **dialogue** from Frank O'Connor's short story, *The Genius*:

- Larry is all of six years old and very clever. He 'badly wants to know where babies come from'. His problem is that none of the adults in his life want to tell a six-year-old the truth and 'rob' him of his 'innocence'.
'It was a moonlit November night, and lights were burning in the little cottages along the road when Una brought me home. On the road outside she said, "This is where little John Joe was killed."
There was nothing remarkable about the spot, and I saw no chance of acquiring any useful information.
"Was it a Ford or a Morris?" I asked, more out of politeness than anything else.
"I don't know," she replied with smouldering anger. "It was Donegan's old car. They can never look where they're going, the old shows!"
"Our Lord probably wanted him," I said perfunctorily.
"I dare say he did," Una replied, though she showed no particular conviction. "That old fool, Donegan – I could kill him whenever I think of it."
"You should get your mother to make you another," I suggested helpfully.
"Make me a what?" Una exclaimed in consternation.
"Make you another brother," I repeated earnestly. "It's quite easy, really. She has an engine in her tummy, and all your daddy has to do is to start it with his starting handle."
"Cripes!" Una said, and clasped her hand over her mouth in an explosion of giggles. "Imagine me telling her that!"

QUICK TEST

The Genius

1. Give a sentence or a word that suggests that Larry has the vocabulary of a 'genius'.

2. Point out a sentence that shows that Larry is self-absorbed.

3. Why is Larry naïve about the facts of life?

4. Give a phrase or word of dialect that suggests that the story is set in Ireland.

5. Which type of narrator can see and know the most?

5. A third-person narrator.
4. 'The old shows', 'Donegan' and 'cripes'.
3. He is only six years old; the adults in his life do not think it is time for someone so young to know the facts of life so they have made up all kinds of answers to his questions.
2. Again, any of Larry's early sentences would do here.
1. Any of the early sentences and the word 'perfunctorily' would hardly be expected of a six-year-old.

THEMES, MOOD AND ATMOSPHERE AND THE SIMILARITIES AND DIFFERENCES OF NOVELS AND STORIES (EN2)

THEMES

Themes are <u>ideas</u> or <u>messages</u> that writers explore in their stories. The novel is a <u>form</u> of writing that allows writers to use more than one <u>theme</u>.

• In *Roll of Thunder Hear My Cry* (1976, Mildred D. Taylor) explores the <u>theme</u> of growing up and the coming of age of its main character, Cassie Logan. She experiences racism in 1930s' Mississippi, despite her family's best efforts to shield her from its worst aspects. Among other <u>themes</u>, the novel also examines <u>the characters' attachment to the land, family roots,</u> <u>independence</u> and the <u>self-respect</u> that comes from owning parcels of land.

MOOD AND ATMOSPHERE

Writers try to create a <u>mood and atmosphere</u> in stories and novels to illuminate the <u>feelings</u> and <u>actions</u> of their characters. <u>Mood</u> and <u>atmosphere</u>, through the skilful use of description, help set the <u>tone</u> for a piece of writing; this creates a frame of mind for the reader and a sense of expectation of what is to follow. <u>Mood</u> <u>and</u> <u>atmosphere</u> can be achieved by using the following <u>literary</u> <u>effects</u>:

• careful choice of words (<u>diction</u>) which helps suggest an <u>atmosphere</u> and <u>tone</u>
• the <u>length</u> and <u>variety</u> of <u>sentences</u>; short ones can suggest tension
• <u>repetition</u> in sentences of words and phrases
• <u>monologues</u> (speaking to oneself); <u>dreams</u> and <u>day-dreams</u> are good ways of revealing the <u>motives</u> and <u>desires</u> of characters
• <u>similes</u>
• <u>metaphors</u>
• <u>personification</u>
• <u>oxymorons</u>
• <u>alliteration</u>
• <u>assonance</u>
• <u>motifs</u> (<u>words</u>, <u>ideas</u> <u>and</u> <u>imagery</u> which recur in texts)
• the use of the <u>senses</u>: <u>sound, touch, sight, smell and touch</u>
• through the <u>tone</u> of the <u>narrator</u> and his or her <u>closeness</u> to, or <u>distance</u> from, the <u>action</u>.

Examiner's Top Tip
Choose a passage that moves you from a text that you are reading and try to work out how the writer created the mood and atmosphere of the passage.

COMPARING NOVELS AND STORIES

- Both have <u>plots</u> and <u>stories</u>.
- Both may include <u>dialogue</u>.
- Both have <u>characters</u>.
- Both set out <u>themes</u> and <u>ideas</u>.

Short stories differ from novels in that they:
- are usually based upon a <u>specific</u> <u>incident</u> or <u>point</u> in <u>time</u>
- usually have just <u>one</u> main plot and they have no space for <u>sub-plots</u> or <u>sub-texts</u>.

- have <u>less</u> <u>description</u> because there is less space: any <u>description</u> used needs to be <u>economical</u> <u>and</u> <u>essential</u> as it has to add meaning to a story.
- use <u>striking</u> <u>details</u>.
- sometimes have more <u>fragmented</u> <u>dialogue</u>
- include <u>fewer</u> <u>characters</u> who do and say more in less space than characters in novels.

An example of <u>mood</u> <u>and</u> <u>atmosphere</u> from chapter 40 of *Far From The Madding Crowd* (1874) by Thomas Hardy:
- Fanny Robin is weak, exhausted, pregnant and alone, as she tries to walk the final miles to Casterbridge to meet her selfish, deceitful lover, Sergeant Troy. Notice how Hardy's <u>third-person</u> <u>narrator</u> emphatically portrays Fanny's <u>feelings</u> <u>of</u> <u>isolation</u> <u>and</u> <u>despair</u> through the use of <u>imagery</u> <u>of</u> <u>light</u> <u>and</u> <u>dark,</u> Fanny's <u>monologue</u>, <u>sound</u>, <u>diction</u> and <u>general</u> <u>description</u>.

ON CASTERBRIDGE HIGHWAY

For a considerable time the woman walked on. Her steps became feebler, and she strained her eyes to look afar upon the naked road, now indistinct amid the penumbrae of night. At length her onward walk dwindled to the merest totter, and she opened a gate within which was a haystack. Underneath this she sat down and presently slept. When the woman awoke it was to find herself in the depths of a moonless and starless night. A heavy unbroken crust of cloud stretched across the sky, shutting out every speck of heaven; and a distant halo which hung over the town of Casterbridge was visible against the black concave, the luminosity appearing the brighter by its great contrast with the circumscribing darkness. Towards this weak, soft glow the woman turned her eyes.

'If I could only get there!' she said. 'Meet him the day after tomorrow: God help me! Perhaps I shall be in my grave before then. '

A manor-house clock from the far depths of shadow struck the hour, one, in a small, attenuated tone. After midnight the voice of a clock seems to lose in breadth as much as in length, and to diminish its sonorousness to a thin falsetto. Afterwards a light – two lights – arose from the remote shade, and grew larger. A carriage rolled along the road, and passed the gate. It probably contained some late diners-out. The beams from one lamp shone for a moment upon the crouching woman, and threw her face into vivid relief. The face was young in the groundwork, old in the finish; the general contours were flexuous and childlike, but the finer lineaments had begun to be sharp and thin. The pedestrian stood up, apparently with revived determination, and looked around. The road appeared to be familiar to her, and she carefully scanned the fence as she slowly walked along. Presently there became visible a dim white shape; it was another milestone. She drew her fingers across its face to feel the marks.

'Two more!' she said.

QUICK TEST

Read the passage from Thomas Hardy's novel carefully before you answer these questions.

1. Give a sentence or word that suggests that Larry has the vocabulary of a 'genius'.

2. What does 'naked road' suggest about the woman's situation?

3. Select a few words or a phrase that seems to indicate that the woman is taking her final walk and seems to be going to heaven.

4. What may be suggested by the inclusion of the chimes of the manor-house clock?

5. Why is the woman's speech sadly ironic?

5. She speaks the truth about dying; she is unaware that Sergeant Troy has married Bathsheba and has just passed her by

4. The clock is personified with 'voice', as it, too, seems to lose in breadth as in length. Its feeble chimes are said to 'diminish' to 'a thin falsetto' after sounding 'midnight'. The description of the personified clock adds to the atmosphere as the desperation of Fanny's final hours is increased through Hardy's skilful use of sound as well as light

3. The 'weak, soft glow' of the 'halo' that hangs over the town of Casterbridge contrasts with the darkness surrounding the woman. It is as if she is dying and heading towards a heavenly light

2. That she is alone, vulnerable and in the open; there is no one to help her

1. Any of the early sentences or the word 'perfunctorily' would hardly be expected from a child

A WIDE READING CATCH-UP ASSIGNMENT

Compare and contrast each main pair of older and younger female characters from the following stories: *The Withered Arm* (1888) by Thomas Hardy and *The Darkness Out There* (1986) by Penelope Liveley. (EN2)

Examiner's Top Tip
Remember that 'to compare' means 'state what is similar' and 'to contrast' means 'explain what is different'.

THE DARKNESS OUT THERE (1986)

Refer to the notes on the characters on pages 82–83 to help you with your essay.

Points on the setting, historical and social context:

- The story was included in Penelope Lively's book, *Pack of Cards and Other Stories*, published in the middle of Margaret Thatcher's term as prime minister.

- It was a period during which the individual was seen as more important than society; it was also a time when privatisation and private enterprise was more highly valued than public services. Social services were cut back in order to reward those in work with lower taxes. People were encouraged to buy their own homes and, on the whole, they had more money to spend.

- It is in this context that Sandra, who is somewhat conventional in outlook, and Kerry, who probably comes from a council estate, perform a similar function to Gertrude Lodge from Hardy's novel written nearly a hundred years before. However, one thing remains constant: there was very little social provision made by the government when Hardy published his story in 1888 and even less during the period in which Hardy's short story is set, 1819–25.

- The main setting is Packer's End, a spooky wood near Clacton in Essex, through which Sandra and Kerry make their way to Mrs Rutter's 'Nether Cottage'. The name of the cottage carries associations of evil. It is as if it is in 'the bowels of the earth'.

- The young characters in the story are town or city dwellers from Essex and are different from Hardy's characters that live in a fictional hamlet called Holmstoke in rural Dorset.

- Sandra may be fearful as she walks through Packer's End yet she has greater freedom of movement than the female characters in Hardy's story. Sandra's father drives a Ford Escort and she aspires to be a secretary. These characters are stereotypical of the Essex men and women who epitomised the type of people whose individualistic aspirations gave Mrs. Thatcher her electoral successes. On the other hand, Kerry already works part-time as a mechanic and wants to follow this skilled working-class trade when he leaves school.

- Most superstitious beliefs in Lively's story have been relegated to early childhood. Sandra no longer believes that Packer's End is filled with 'witches and wolves'. It is the present-day fears of strangers, rape, and ghosts who 'chatter on their radios' from the wreck of a Second World War German plane, that fill the thoughts of these modern characters. Evil is experienced not through witchcraft, as with Hardy, but through people's deeds – or lack of them. The 'darkness' is not 'out there' in the woods but in people's hearts.

THE WITHERED ARM (1888)

Points on the setting, historical and social context:

- Hardy wrote this story in the 1880s and it was published in 1888. Like most of his novels and stories it is set in the deepest countryside of Wessex (Wiltshire and Dorset). There is a strong hint of threat and evil with the nearby 'Egdon Heath, whose dark countenance' (face) is 'visible in the distance'.

- Hardy's third-person narrator shows through the dialogue between Gertrude Lodge and Conjuror Trendle that the final event in the story takes place in 1825. Conjuror Trendle tells Getrude to go to a local jail in good time for the next hanging to cure her 'withered arm': 'The last I sent was in '13 – near twelve years ago.'

- The narrator allows the reader insight into the deeper superstitions of an earlier period and the narrator also makes it plain that hanging was considered as an unremarkably routine, local event that was often attended by interested spectators.

- At the time, poorly paid labourers had demanded better pay and some had joined secret societies to force the issue with the employers; some groups had burned hay-ricks, barns and other out-buildings in various parts of rural England to pressurise farmers and employers into paying them a living wage. Britain's rulers may also have feared the relatively recent example of the French Revolution. Interestingly, Hardy's father told him about a boy who was hanged after being found staring at a burning hay-rick. Hardy's father also took Thomas as a boy to watch a public hanging. One of those hanged was a woman. This probably left a lasting impression on Hardy because his most famous character, Tess of the D'Urbervilles, dies on the gallows.

- Women in this rural society were either tied to the land like Rhoda or to their husbands like Gertrude. Furthermore, women had relatively few rights of property and movement and therefore enjoyed relatively little freedom.

- The story reveals the life, beliefs and values of a countryside community. The story was published in the widely sold *Blackwoods Magazine* in January 1888. Stories that included supernatural tales, such as this one, were popular with the reading public in late-Victorian Britain.

Examiner's Top Tip
Use a variety of sentences in your essay and a range of connective words to clarify your ideas.

AN ESSAY PLAN

- Write down the essay title in all drafts to keep your answer focused. Always write a first draft for course-work essays.
- Remember to read the notes on the characters on (pages 82–85) because they are designed to help you with your essay. As you introduce each character, write a brief paragraph about their historical and social context (their background); or include these aspects in your comments on the characters wherever it seems appropriate to do so.

GIVE THE BACKGROUND, APPEARANCES AND RESIDENCES OF THE CHARACTERS
- Compare and contrast the background and appearance of Gertrude and Sandra.
- Compare and contrast the background, appearance and residences of the older characters, Rhoda Brook and Mrs Rutter.

WHAT IS LEARNED BY THE YOUNGER CHARACTERS?
- Compare and contrast what is learned by Sandra and Gertrude.

EXPLAIN THEIR CHARACTERS AND WHAT SHAPED THEM
- What is similar and dissimilar about the characters of Gertrude and Sandra?
- Make a few comparisons and contrasts on the characters of Rhoda Brook and Mrs Rutter.

WHAT IS SIMILAR AND WHAT IS DIFFERENT ABOUT THE MOTIVATION OF EACH CHARACTER?
- Compare and contrast the hopes and desires of Gertrude and Sandra.
- Make a few comparisons and contrasts on the motives of Rhoda and Mrs Rutter.

CONCLUSION
- Conclude by giving your views on the stories and what you learned from writing this essay.

SANDRA
The Darkness Out There

Notes on Sandra from Penelope Lively's *The Darkness Out There* (1986) and Gertrude Lodge from Thomas Hardy's story, *The Withered Arm* (1888). The notes detail their appearances, characters, motivations and what they learn. (EN2)

SANDRA FROM THE DARKNESS OUT THERE

GENERAL DESCRIPTION

- **She is 16, pretty and lower-middle class**. She wants to be a secretary when she leaves school. Her father drives a Ford Escort and she lives in Essex. She is conventional and ambitious. She considers herself to be a cut above Kerry. Sandra always uses standard English. Kerry does not.

SANDRA'S CHARACTER

- **She is charitable because she is doing a good deed to help Mrs Rutter through 'The Good Neighbours Club'**. However, she may be doing this because it is a craze and considered by others to be the right thing to do.

- **Like Gertrude in Hardy's story she is squeamish** because she does not want to hear about the German plane at Packer's End. She thinks that she is past the stage of **superstition** and the belief in witches and fairies. Yet she is fearful of Packer's End: its darkness and its associated horror stories of rape and death frighten her.

- **She is conventional and prejudiced** because she judges Kerry and other characters by their appearance. She does not like his '**black licked down hair and slitty eyes**'.

AIMS AND AMBITIONS

- **Sandra dreams of an ideal married life:**
'One day she would have a place in the country, but not like this [Mrs Rutter's cottage]. A little white house peeping over a hill, with a stream at the bottom of a crisp green lawn and an orchard with old apple trees and a brown pony. And she would walk in the long grass in this orchard in a straw hat with these two children, a boy and a girl, children with fair shiny hair like hers, and there'd be this man.'

LEARNING FROM EXPERIENCE

- **Sandra learns that you can misjudge people**: Mrs Rutter and Kerry. Kerry's reaction to the disclosure of Mrs Rutter's cold-hearted and vengeful behaviour shows him to be a decent, good person.

- **Sandra gains experience in time to help her**, whereas Gertrude gains her experience too late. Sandra learns that **'the darkness' is 'out there' but it is not in the woods but in people's hearts**. She therefore learns that '**everything is not as it appears**', and by doing so, she grows up.

> **Examiner's Top Tip**
> Do not try to include all your information in essays. Select points that are relevant for the question and prove them with sufficient evidence from the text. Remember to comment on your points where you can.

GERTRUDE LODGE
The Withered Arm

GERTRUDE FROM THE WITHERED ARM

GENERAL DESCRIPTION

- She is a gentlewoman who is married to wealthy Farmer Lodge.

- She is pretty and young. She arrives in Holmstoke with Farmer Lodge as his new, 19-year-old bride. She is a middle-class young 'lady' whose gentility is reflected by the softness of hands that have never been used for manual labour.

GERTRUDE'S CHARACTER

- She is genuinely charitable because she gives Rhoda Brook's son a pair of boots. He tells Rhoda, 'She gives away things to other folks in the Meads besides us.'

- Gertrude is trusting, naive and innocent. This can be seen from her reaction to the curious stare that Rhoda's son gives her as she rides by with her husband in a 'gig'. Gertrude comments, 'I think the poor boy may have looked at us in the hope we might relieve him of his heavy load, rather than from curiosity.' She is not, as yet, superstitious in the story. She also seems innocent because she is described as 'a girl' whose 'face was fresh in colour'. It is 'soft and evanescent, like the light under a heap of rose petals'. Gertrude is unaware that she is filling Rhoda's place as Farmer Lodge's bride.

- She is squeamish. Gertrude has a strong aversion to the cure suggested by Trendle of touching the neck of a freshly hanged man so that it may 'turn the blood'.

AIMS AND AMBITIONS

- Gertrude's arm becomes increasingly disfigured because of an unconscious spell cast by Rhoda Brook while each slept.

- Gertrude wants to regain the love of her husband and seem 'whole' again. She becomes increasingly desperate for a cure.

- She learns from Conjuror Trendle that Rhoda disfigured her. He tells her, 'Tis the work of an enemy' and he shows Gertrude the face of the person who disfigured her in a glass filled with the white of an egg. As she becomes superstitious and irritable she learns about the background of Rhoda and her son. She becomes obsessive in her desire to become beautiful again. Her desire, and the knowledge of what happened to her, leads her into having a mania for superstition and for magic potions and spells, and drives her on her quest for Trendle's suggested cure. She: 'Well neigh longed for the death of a fellow creature. Instead of her formal prayers each night her unconscious prayer was, "O Lord, hang some guilty or innocent person soon"'.

- Gertrude's longing to be cured is similar to the longing and obsession that Rhoda Brook had at the beginning of the story when Rhoda pictures Gertrude through her imagination, without actually seeing her.

LEARNING FROM EXPERIENCE

- She is cured and gains knowledge from her experience. But it is too late to help her!

MRS RUTTER
The Darkness Out There

Notes on Mrs Rutter from Penelope Lively's *The Darkness Out There* (1986) and Rhoda Brook from Thomas Hardy's *The Withered Arm* (1888). The notes detail the women's appearances, residences, characters and motivations. (EN2)

MRS RUTTER FROM THE DARKNESS OUT THERE

GENERAL DESCRIPTION

- Mrs Rutter is an old-age pensioner. She seems happy-go-lucky but her 'eyes are as quick as mice'. She looks shapeless, as if 'composed of circles, a cottage-loaf of a woman'.
- She has the appearance of a witch from a fairy-tale. She lives in 'Nether Cottage', deep in the haunted wood of Packer's End somewhere in Essex, not far from Clapton.

CHARACTER

- Her character has been affected by losing her husband early in their marriage.
- She is superstitious because she says 'touch wood' and 'cross fingers'. She is also manipulative because she flatters Sandra: 'I suppose you have lots of boyfriends.' She implies that Kerry is 'all sorts'.
- Mrs Rutter's happy-go-lucky chatter overlays the bitterness that she feels about the loss of her married life and being denied any children: 'It's been a loss that.' She became a young war-widow when her husband died early in the Second World War. She poignantly remembers that she made her own wedding dress. She muses that it is 'sad that Pat Hammond never married'.
- She seems unconscious of her previous coldness and cruelty. She is unaware of any hypocrisy. Ironically, she repeatedly tells her visitors, 'I have a lot of sympathy for young people.'

MOTIVATION

- She is motivated by feelings of revenge.
- Mrs Rutter wanted revenge against the Germans for the loss of her husband and making her a young widow. She thinks that the deaths of the young pilots' were 'tit-for-tat'.

- She is cold and not squeamish. She claims that she was never 'squeamish' and shows her vengeful, cold nature by doing nothing to help the young German pilot who dies a lingering death. She says of him, 'Good riddance to bad rubbish' and 'He must have been a tough bastard'. Rather than help the pilot she selfishly wanted to get home out of the rain.
- Her revenge upon the Germans is at first opportune and later calculated. Rhoda Brook's 'revenge' on Gertrude, in which she received a withered arm, is unconscious and not calculated.

RHODA BROOK
The Withered Arm

RHODA BROOK FROM THE WITHERED ARM

GENERAL DESCRIPTION

- Rhoda Brook <u>is a 'poor lorn milkmaid' in</u> her <u>early thirties</u>. She is 'thin', 'worn' and 'tall'. She lives with her 12-year-old son, whose natural father is Farmer Lodge, in a 'lonely spot' near Egdon Heath. A place 'whose dark countenance was visible in the distance'. Farmer Lodge ignores his natural son.

CHARACTER

- <u>Her character relates to her circumstances as an abandoned woman</u>; her evil-doing is unconscious; she reacts like a woman who has been supplanted by another and who has to live with local opinion.

- <u>Rhoda questions her 'malignant' powers</u>. Unsure of her powers she wonders, 'O, can it be . . . that I exercise a malignant power over people against my own will?'. <u>Her revenge is not a conscious one</u>.

- She is caught between <u>fear and fascination</u> as she reluctantly leads Gertrude to Conjuror Trendle. Locals inform Gertrude that Rhoda would 'know more about the movements' of a 'clever man' than anyone else. This is because it is locally thought that '<u>a sorceress would know the whereabouts of an exorcist</u>'.

- To a certain extent, Rhoda trades on her reputation: 'There was a horrid fascination at times in becoming instrumental in throwing such possible light on her own character as would reveal her to be something greater in the occult world than she had ever herself suspected.'

MOTIVATION

- Her <u>motivation</u> stems from being <u>passed over</u> by Farmer Lodge.

- Rhoda becomes <u>obsessive</u> about Gertrude's <u>appearance</u> and anxious to know all about the woman who supplanted her.

- She uses <u>West Country dialect</u> as she tells her son to give 'a look' at the new wife and report all he sees. She wants above all to know of any imperfections in Mrs Lodge.

- Rhoda 'stares into the fire' and develops a '<u>mental image</u>' of Mrs Lodge as 'realistic as any photograph' before she goes to bed. She dreams of Gertrude visiting her and mocking her with her 'wedding ring'. In her dream Rhoda feels 'suffocated' by Gertrude. It is as if Gertrude is sitting on Rhoda's chest. Rhoda leaves the imprint of her fingers on the arm of the 'spectre' as she 'whirls it backward to the floor'.

- She sees the '<u>meaning of what Satan showed</u>' her in a '<u>vision</u>', and angrily seizes Gertrude's arm and throws her against a wall as Rhoda and Farmer Lodge claim the body of their executed son: 'Hussy – to come between us and our child now!'

EXAM QUESTIONS - Use the questions to test your progress. Check your answers on page 95.

How to Study Novels and Short Stories

1. Give three types of texts that you can compare.

....

2. When must the older text date before?

....

3. What is the other important rule for the older text?

....

4. What is the historical context of a text?

....

5. Are you assessed on reading or writing?

....

6. What does 'plot' mean?

....

7. What does it mean to 'contrast'?

....

8. Explain the term 'genre'.

....

9. What is meant by a 'writer's craft'?

....

10. Explain what irony means.

....

11. What are 'transitions'?

....

12. Give two types of themes that you may write about in your assignments.

....

Literary Technique: Narrators, Characterisation and Dialogue

13. What are the main styles of narration?

....

14. From which viewpoint does a first-person narrator tell a story?

....

15. Does the author believe what a narrator believes?

....

16. What type of narrator can see most in a story?

....

17. Give three ways of understanding a character.

....

18. What does 'eponymous' mean?

....

19. What is meant by the terms 'flat' and 'round' characters?

....

20. Define what dialogue means.

....

21. Why do writers use dialogue?

....

22. Briefly explain the rules for how dialogue should be set out on the page.

....

23. What is a monologue?

....

24. How can dialogue help you learn more about characters?

....

Themes, Atmosphere and the Differences between Novels and Stories

25. Identify three similarities in novels and short stories.

....

26. Point out three differences between short stories and novels.

....

27. Why do short stories concentrate on mainly one plot?

....

28. Point out three ways in which writers create mood and atmosphere in their stories.

....

29. What is 'diction'?

....

30. Mood and atmosphere sets up a frame of mind and an expectation of what is to follow in a text. True or false?

....

31. Mood and atmosphere can be achieved through the skilful use of description or imagery. True or false?

....

32. Imagery is only used for poetry and not in novels or short stories. True or false?

....

33. Explain the difference between alliteration and assonance.

....

34. What is a theme?

....

35. Give one example of a theme that can be linked with the historical context of a novel or a story.

....

36. Briefly sum up the difference between a short story and a novel.

....

How did you do?

1–9	correct	.start again
10–19	correct	.getting there
20–29	correct	.good work
30–36	correct	.excellent

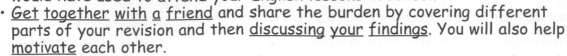

ARE YOU ON STUDY LEAVE?

- The <u>secret of success</u> is to do a <u>little and often</u> every day. Assign yourself <u>set times</u> to do your revision. Why not stick to the times you would have used to attend your English lessons in school?
- <u>Get together with a friend</u> and share the burden by covering different parts of your revision and then <u>discussing your findings</u>. You will also help <u>motivate</u> each other.
- For essay plans <u>brainstorm</u> your ideas and then <u>write numbers</u> around your <u>brainstormed plan</u> so that you can <u>list your ideas in the best order</u>. This will give your essay <u>a logical, fluent</u> structure. Ask a friend to mark your work and correct any <u>punctuation mistakes</u>. Improve your <u>proof-reading skills</u> by marking the work of friends.

PLANNING AND READING IN EXAMS

- <u>Do not panic</u>! Channel all your <u>nervous energy</u> and <u>adrenaline</u> into your exam. If you are answering questions on poetry, <u>find the questions that apply to you</u> and do the ones that you think that you can answer best.
- <u>Question the question</u>. <u>Read the questions very carefully and underline key words and phrases</u>. Think about these as you read your passages.
- <u>Read through</u> written passages <u>twice</u>: <u>firstly</u> to get <u>the gist</u> of the <u>meaning</u> and <u>then for deeper understanding</u>. Carefully read the passages and <u>note the development of arguments and ideas</u> as well as how they are expressed by <u>underlining words</u> or by <u>making short, phrase-like notes</u>.
- <u>Brainstorm a brief five-point</u> (or so) <u>plan</u> and then <u>re-number your points</u> in the order in that you will need to write them (this will help your <u>structure</u>).

WHEN YOU WRITE EXAM ANSWERS

- <u>Do not waste time with long introductions</u> – get straight into your answer with only <u>a brief introduction</u>, setting out your answer and remembering to use <u>standard English</u>. That is, make sure that your <u>writing is formal</u> and <u>avoid abbreviations</u>, unless you are asked to use <u>dialect</u>.
- Show your understanding of texts by <u>reading between the lines</u> and by <u>putting information in your own words</u>. Remember to use <u>brief quotations as evidence</u> for your points and <u>integrate them within your writing</u>. Constantly refer back to the question, when writing, and ask yourself, 'Am I being <u>relevant</u> here?' and, 'Am I using <u>key words from the question</u> in my answer.'
- <u>Add points to your plan while writing</u> in case you forget them. Your brain is remarkable because you can think of two things at once. Do not lose track of good ideas as you write your answers. Simply <u>break off from your answer</u> and <u>add</u> the necessary points to your plan.
- Be <u>ruthless</u> and divide your time <u>sensibly</u> according to the marks at stake for each <u>question</u>. Do not get bogged down looking for an extra one or two marks when there is a <u>fresh question</u> with <u>several marks</u> at stake. You should be trying to <u>average</u> a high number of marks for each question. Do not unbalance your effort by trying to get the maximum mark for any single question. You must <u>spread your effort</u> and <u>aim for an overall mark in your answers</u>. That is a <u>successful technique</u>.
- <u>Your aim is to build up marks in each answer</u> and to share your effort efficiently. A paragraph or so with bullet points is fine for six marks but you will need <u>several paragraphs</u> for a 26-mark question. Again, be careful not spend <u>too long</u> on questions with few marks at stake.
- <u>Managing your time is crucial in exams</u>. Allow yourself five to 10 minutes to check your work through for errors of <u>sense</u>, <u>spelling</u> and <u>punctuation</u>. Ask yourself, 'What errors do I usually make?'

FIVE POINTS TO REMEMBER ON THE WORDING OF WRITING EXAM QUESTIONS

In exam questions to:
1. <u>explain</u> means to show <u>knowledge</u> <u>and</u> <u>understanding</u> by giving a <u>detailed</u> <u>account</u> of something
2. <u>describe</u> means to set forth the <u>characteristics</u> <u>or</u> <u>details</u> of something
3. <u>argue</u> is to maintain <u>a stand-point</u> through logic as you would in an essay
4. <u>inform</u> means to <u>show</u> <u>an</u> <u>understanding</u> <u>of</u> <u>something</u> <u>by</u> <u>giving</u> <u>a</u> <u>clear</u> <u>account</u> <u>of</u> <u>it</u> to someone else
5. Advise is similar to inform: it means to <u>teach</u> someone or a particular audience something as clearly as you can.

EXAM TECHNIQUE AND GENERAL ADVICE

FIVE POINTS TO REMEMBER ABOUT WORDS AND PHRASES IN READING EXAM QUESTIONS

1. <u>Use</u> <u>of</u> <u>language</u> means <u>word</u> <u>choices</u>, <u>emotive</u> <u>words</u> <u>and</u> <u>phrases</u> to affect the audience, <u>description</u>, <u>persuasive phrases</u>, <u>imagery</u>, <u>alliteration</u>, etc. Avoid saying that the language used 'is very good' which suggests you do not know what to say.
2. <u>Style</u> <u>of</u> <u>presentation</u> means <u>how the text is set out</u>. Think about the <u>text's</u> <u>form</u>. For instance, is it a letter or a newspaper article? Think about the use of <u>underlining</u>, <u>bullet</u> <u>points</u>, <u>statistics</u>, <u>graphs</u> and <u>pictures</u>. How do each of these <u>devices</u> express <u>meaning</u> and aid <u>understanding</u>?
3. The <u>attitude</u> <u>to</u> <u>the</u> <u>reader</u> is the <u>'tone of voice'</u> adopted by the writer. Is it, for example, <u>polite</u>, <u>ironic</u>, <u>formal</u>, <u>informal</u>, <u>serious</u>, <u>comic</u>, <u>academic</u>, <u>sarcastic</u>, etc. The <u>tone</u> a writer chooses is always important for the <u>purpose</u> of any piece of writing.
4. <u>Convey</u> means <u>to</u> <u>get</u> <u>across</u>. For example, 'How does the writer convey a sense of . . .'
5. <u>Compare</u> <u>and</u> <u>contrast</u> means: 'What is <u>similar</u>?' and 'What is <u>different</u>?'

PRACTICE QUESTIONS

Questions for 30-minute exam practice for the poetry sections of the exam.

Poets in the English National Heritage

1. Write about two poems that interested you. Explain why.

2. Examine the presentation of characters in at least two poems.

Poetry From Other Cultures

1. Compare two poems that are linked by a similar theme.

2. Compare and contrast two poems from this section.

Examiner's Top Tip
Use your time effectively. In the NEAB Paper 1 you have two hours to get 108 marks. Excluding planning time, that works out at almost a mark a minute.

THE READING SECTIONS

WHAT YOU SHOULD HAVE REVISED

- Find the <u>relevant</u> stories or poems that you have been studying in class. <u>Do</u> <u>not</u> <u>write</u> <u>about</u> <u>poems</u> <u>and</u> <u>poets</u> <u>that</u> <u>you</u> <u>have</u> <u>not</u> <u>studied</u>. This seems an obvious point yet a number of pupils each year write about poems, etc. that they have never studied. The two poetry sections combined are worth <u>15%</u> of your final mark.

- Remember that time will be <u>limited</u>. For example, in the NEAB Exam <u>you</u> <u>only</u> <u>have</u> <u>half</u> <u>an</u> <u>hour</u> for each exam to answer the questions for your prepared poetry sections on:

  - <u>Carol</u> <u>Ann</u> <u>Duffy</u>, <u>Simon</u> <u>Armitage</u> or <u>Ted</u> <u>Hughes</u>
  - '<u>Poetry</u> <u>From</u> <u>Other</u> <u>Cultures</u>'

- Other exam boards will also set short time limits on their <u>pre-released</u> <u>reading</u> <u>materials</u>, so it is important to be <u>relevant</u> in your answers and to <u>use</u> <u>appropriate</u> <u>evidence</u> <u>for</u> <u>your</u> <u>points</u>.

- You should have revised <u>key</u> <u>themes</u> <u>that</u> <u>link</u> <u>your</u> <u>poems</u> <u>or</u> <u>stories</u> <u>together</u>. The best way to see which texts go together is to <u>produce</u> <u>a</u> <u>chart</u> <u>with</u> <u>the</u> <u>poems</u> <u>down</u> <u>one</u> <u>side</u> <u>and</u> <u>the</u> <u>themes</u> <u>at</u> <u>the</u> <u>top</u>. Briefly point out any connections between the themes in your squares; you will then see which texts to pair up and write about in exams. For example, look again at pages 66–67 on Carol Ann Duffy in this book for <u>themes</u> that can be made into a chart.

WHEN YOU BEGIN WRITING

- Write about <u>links</u> between the poems or stories and <u>show</u> <u>your</u> <u>awareness</u> <u>of</u> <u>the</u> <u>main</u> <u>similarities</u> <u>and</u> <u>differences</u>.
- If you are doing the <u>Foundation</u> paper use the <u>bullet</u> <u>points</u> which your exam board has provided for you under your question. You may not be able to answer all the bullet points in the time allowed. You should then aim to do <u>three</u> <u>out</u> <u>of</u> <u>four</u> bullet points and <u>do</u> <u>them</u> <u>as</u> <u>well</u> <u>as</u> <u>you</u> <u>can</u>. Examiners are looking for <u>understanding</u>, <u>knowledge</u> and <u>relevance</u>, rather than long answers in which pupils try to say everything that they know.
- The advice is the same for anyone doing the <u>Higher</u> paper, only <u>you</u> <u>have</u> <u>to</u> <u>brain-storm</u> <u>your</u> <u>own</u> <u>four-</u> <u>or</u> <u>five-point</u> <u>plan</u> <u>from</u> <u>the</u> <u>question</u>. You should <u>number</u> <u>the</u> <u>points</u> <u>in</u> <u>your</u> <u>plan</u> afterwards to help you produce a <u>structured</u> and <u>fluent</u> answer. Remember that you cannot, and should not, say everything that you know about your chosen poems. You will probably only use around 25% of your knowledge so it is vital to be <u>relevant</u> and <u>focus</u> your answer on <u>key</u> <u>words</u> <u>and</u> <u>phrases</u> <u>from</u> <u>your</u> <u>question</u>.
- <u>Facts</u> are things that <u>can</u> be <u>proved</u>, for example, 'Chelsea FC won the FA Cup in 2000'.
- Opinions <u>cannot</u> be <u>proved</u> because they are subjective. For example, 'Chelsea FC will win the Premier League for the next three seasons!'
- <u>Be</u> <u>wary</u> <u>of</u> <u>facts</u> <u>dressed</u> <u>up</u> <u>as</u> <u>opinions</u>. For example, 'Chelsea have a policy of buying only foreign players because they have so many of them in their team.'

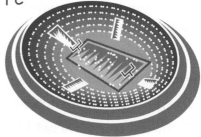

HOW TO ANSWER QUESTIONS ON UNSEEN, NON-FICTION TEXTS DURING YOUR EXAMS (EN2)

- <u>Reading</u>, <u>including</u> <u>the</u> <u>two</u> <u>poetry</u> <u>sections</u>, <u>is</u> <u>worth</u> <u>15%</u> <u>of</u> <u>your</u> <u>final</u> <u>mark</u>. Unseen non-fiction includes: passages, extracts or articles. Once you establish the <u>form</u> <u>and</u> <u>purpose</u> <u>of</u> <u>the</u> <u>writing</u>, you will then be able to produce a more <u>detailed</u> <u>answer</u> <u>in</u> <u>which</u> <u>you</u> <u>later</u> <u>show</u> <u>how</u> <u>a</u> <u>writer</u> <u>either</u> <u>informs</u> <u>or</u> <u>persuades</u> <u>their</u> <u>audience</u>.
- <u>There</u> <u>are</u> <u>three</u> <u>main</u> <u>questions</u> <u>to</u> <u>ask</u> <u>of</u> <u>any</u> <u>text</u>:
1. What kind of writing is this? Is the writing meant to <u>entertain</u>, <u>inform</u>, <u>persuade</u>, etc.
2. What is the <u>form</u> of the writing? Is it <u>an</u> <u>article</u>, <u>leaflet</u>, <u>letter</u>, <u>biography</u>, etc. Does the writer use the <u>first</u> or <u>third</u> person? The <u>second-person</u> form of <u>'you'</u> is often used in junk mail. Remember that <u>layout</u> and <u>images</u> are an important way of <u>getting</u> <u>messages</u> <u>across</u>. Be prepared to comment on their effectiveness, especially when you are asked to <u>compare</u> one text with another.
3. What does the text <u>mean</u> to you? What are your <u>motives</u> for reading this text? Do you <u>share</u> its values? How will you <u>interpret</u> it? What does it make you <u>think</u>?

In other words:
1. **What is the writer trying to say?**
2. **What means does he or she employ towards effective communication?**
3. **How successful is the writer in achieving his or her aims?**

TIPS ON PERSUASIVE TECHNIQUES

Look again at the Media pages of this book on 'How To Analyse A Media Text' for fuller advice on <u>persuasive</u> <u>techniques</u>. You could use any variation of them in your answers on passages or in your own piece of writing.

<u>Rhetorical</u> <u>questions</u>: these are designed to <u>involve</u> <u>an</u> <u>audience</u> and make them <u>think</u> about an issue.

<u>Formatting</u>: <u>underlining</u>, <u>bullet</u> <u>points</u>, <u>statistics</u>, <u>the</u> <u>use</u> <u>of</u> <u>colour</u>, <u>capital</u> <u>letters</u>, <u>bold</u> <u>print</u>, graphics and <u>well-chosen</u> <u>pictures</u> <u>with</u> <u>captions</u> can also play an important part in <u>persuading</u> an audience and <u>make</u> <u>information</u> <u>easier</u> <u>to</u> <u>grasp</u>.

<u>Personal</u> <u>testimony</u>: brief quotations from <u>experts</u> or <u>witnesses</u> can be used to <u>verify</u> <u>arguments</u> and make them appear more <u>valid</u>.

<u>Emotive</u> <u>language</u>: words and phrases that can make you <u>feel</u> <u>strongly</u> about someone or something.

<u>Repetition</u>: this is a form of <u>rhetoric</u> in which you <u>repeat key phrases in your</u> <u>arguments</u>. For example:

<u>Firstly</u>, <u>secondly</u>, <u>and</u> <u>thirdly</u> . . . Dr Martin Luther King famously repeated the phrase 'I have a dream' to great effect in his speech for equality outside the White House in 1968.

PERSUASIVE TECHNIQUES ARE PARTICULARLY USEFUL FOR EXAMS

<u>Humour</u>: when this is used in a controlled way to <u>undermine</u> <u>an</u> <u>opposing</u> <u>point</u> <u>of</u> <u>view</u> it can be very effective.

<u>Fonts</u> <u>and</u> <u>type</u> <u>sizes</u>: these are often carefully selected to give points more impact or carry other associations that advertisers would like you to think.

QUICK TEST

1. How much time do you have for your answer in each poetry section?
2. What is the second person and where would you find it?
3. What is a fact?
4. Is this a fact or an opinion: 'Animal experimentation is wrong.'
5. What is emotive language?

5. Words and phrases which are meant to make you feel strongly about something.
4. An opinion.
3. Something that you can prove.
2. You. Mostly in junk mail, sales literature etc.
1. 30 minutes.

HOW TO PRODUCE A PIECE OF WRITING WORTHY OF A HIGH GRADE

You will need to do the following to produce a good answer:
- **Plan** your writing.
- Focus on your **purpose** (what you want your **audience** to know).
- **Consider** **your** **audience** and use an appropriate language and tone.
- **Use** **varied** **sentence** **structure** and punctuation, as well as showing clarity of thought.
- Develop points into logical, well-constructed **paragraphs** with **topic** **sentences**.
- Use a variety of **linking** **words** (conjunctions) to help you signpost your points.
- Show **accuracy** in your **spelling** and **punctuation**.
- **Proof-read** your work and **correct** **it** where necessary. Teachers and examiners love to see evidence of **proof-reading** because it shows that pupils have attained a level of maturity as **independent** **learners**.

WRITING TO ARGUE, PERSUADE OR INSTRUCT

This **is** **worth** **15%** **of** **your** **final** **mark.**

- *Audience and purpose*
  The first thing to do is consider your purpose and then focus on how you can best persuade your particular audience.

- *Form*
  Select an appropriate form: a letter, newspaper article, pamphlet, leaflet, essay, etc.

- *Planning*
  Always plan your writing. A brief brainstormed or mind-mapped plan can later be numbered to help you order and shape your writing.

- *Use appropriate language and register*
  All formal writing needs to be written in standard English.

- *Be convincing*
  If you are writing a letter of complaint try to avoid sounding pompous, strident or foolishly outraged. You must build instead a reasonable case that is based on as much evidence as you can muster.

WRITING TO ADVISE, INFORM, EXPLAIN OR DESCRIBE

This **is** **worth** **15%** **of** **your** **final** **mark.**

- This could be anything from composing a letter informing parents of a school trip to composing a leaflet setting out the dangers of tooth decay for primary school-aged pupils.

- The choice of topic that you will be asked to write about will be determined by the material that you read earlier in the exam. So if you had read articles or information pamphlets on tooth decay, you will have a number of facts, statistics, opinions, arguments and evidence to draw upon. But beware of simply repeating sentences and paragraphs that you have previously read. That is plagiarism. Process the information by putting it in your own words and by giving credit to the other writers by citing (giving) their names and the titles of the articles in your work.

- Foundation papers will help you by providing a brief plan for your writing with helpful advice. If you are taking the higher paper you will then have to brainstorm your own. Remember that writing which is planned is better than that which is unplanned. There is simply more fluency, structure and detail in planned writing. You will also avoid head-scratching in the middle of your exam if you have thought about your writing in the first five to 10 minutes of your answer.

- Exam boards these days are not overly concerned with the form in which pupils' writing is set out: it is what is said and how it is expressed that is more important. In other words, you do not have to worry about making, for instance, a newspaper article look like one. You should try, however, to adopt the written style of a journalist.

PRACTICE QUESTIONS FOR BOTH TYPES OF WRITING IN THE EXAM

You usually get <u>an hour</u> for these sections of the papers. Try some of the following ideas for exam practice at home.

PAPER 1. WRITING TO ARGUE, PERSUADE OR ADVISE
- Argue for or against blood sports or animal experimentation for an audience of your own age.
- Write a pamphlet on the dangers of under-age drinking or smoking for a younger audience.
- Prepare a detailed list of instructions for organising a prize-giving evening for teachers.
- Write an article for young people in which you argue for or against the effects of watching television.

PAPER 2. WRITING TO ADVISE, INFORM, EXPLAIN OR DESCRIBE
- Write an explanation of your favourite hobby for a beginner.
- Describe your ideal teacher.
- Look at sections of magazines that show a day in the life of someone. Write about a typical day in your life and entitle it 'A Life In The Day of . . . '
- Write about an event that changed your outlook on life.

THE WRITING SECTIONS

The two writing sections of the exams are worth 30% of your final mark – 15% in Paper 1 and 15% in Paper 2.

Five Points to Remember
1. You have one hour for each section of writing.
2. Plan your writing. Spend between five to 10 minutes making your plan.
3. Number the points in your plan so that your writing has fluency and structure.
4. Signpost your arguments and points with a variety of connectives.
5. Match your style of writing to your chosen form.

QUICK TEST

1. Why is it important to plan your writing?
2. Should you use abbreviations in your writing?
3. What must you always do once you complete a piece of writing?
4. What are the two main factors to consider when producing a piece of writing for the exam?
5. How much of your final grade depends on the writing sections of the exam?

5. 30%
4. You must consider the purpose and target audience for your writing.
3. Proof-read your work for punctuation, spelling, clarity and sense.
2. No. Stick with standard English. Only use dialect if it is asked for.
1. It will have more detail and be more structured.

93

Punctuation, Speaking and Listening

Punctuation and Sentences

1. You need to punctuate your work so that your readers will fully understand your meaning.
2. Check your answer against page 7. (Award yourself a mark if you got all five.)
3. Jemma, *Great Expectations*, English, the first She, Charles Dickens and Easter.
4. Full stop, semi-colon, colon, exclamation mark and question mark.
5. They join closely related sentences; they separate sets of items in lists when there are commas within the sets or lists.
6. A question to which you do not expect a direct answer. You expect instead that your listener will agree with you.
7. Colons can introduce a list; they can introduce a sentence which expands upon the meaning of the first sentence; they can also introduce long quotations that are separated from the writer's prose.
8. Inverted commas are needed for words spoken; the speech needs to be separated from the rest of the writing by a punctuation mark; it is introduced with a capital letter; you need a new line for each speaker; and each new line should be indented three spaces from the margin.
9. Apostrophes can indicate possession or an abbreviated word or phrase.
10. Before the 's' as with the firemen's equipment.
11. Statements, exclamations, instructions or commands and questions.
12. The main clause is 'I will go to the cinema'. The dependent clause is 'as soon as I have done the washing up'.

Spelling and Expression

13. Spelling phonetically sounding out each syllable:
Look–Cover–Say
Write–Check
Use a dictionary; produce a mnemonic.
14. It is 'i' before 'e' except after 'c'.
15. There is a consonant before the 'y' as with 'city'; so it's 'cities'.
16. There is a vowel before the 'y' as with 'monkey'; so it's 'monkeys'.
17. American spellings: O.K., theater, and humor. British spellings: centre, tyre and cancelled.
18. Beginning, appearance, interested, grammar, tongue, definitely, necessity, rhythm, sentence.
19. Synonyms are words that mean the same. An example is 'respond' and 'answer'.
20. Homophones are words that are different yet sound the same. For instance, 'whether' and 'weather'.
21. Connective words link phrases, sentences and paragraphs together.
22. To help signpost ideas and arguments so that readers can follow what you mean.

23. Paragraphs break up forbidding chunks of text and make meaning clear. Writers need them to organise their main points and ideas.
24. The topic sentence is the main sentence in a paragraph. The remaining sentences expand on its meaning.
25. 'Control' is the ability to write sentences and paragraphs of appropriate length with control over expression. Word choices and punctuation will also be appropriate and accurate.
26. Because.

Speaking and Listening

27. Three.
28. Single, paired and group orals.
29. Local speech particular to an area. It is informal speech.
30. Cockney, Geordie, Scouse, Brummie. There are many others!
31. Formal English used by teachers, doctors, lawyers, in business, etc.
32. Use local dialect with your friends and family. This is because it is friendly and informal; use standard English in formal situations to people with whom you are doing business and do not know.
33. You should note details such as the type of oral and the topic; you will need the date, some notes on your preparation; you should record how the oral went by making a self-assessment so you can set targets for your next oral.
34. Non-verbal language such as eye contact, hand gestures, etc.
35. Register is the tone you adopt when addressing various audiences; for example you should speak to a judge than you would to a friend.
36. We are being ironic if the tone of our voices implies the opposite meaning of words we use.
37. Good listeners have better, more complex conversations. They have good turn-taking skills too.
38. To 'work out', to 'unpick', to 'unravel'.
39. Debates, topical issues in the news; or an issue that came out of a class text.
40. You are assessed on your ability to talk, not to read. Long, written passages prevent fluency in speech because of the temptation to look at them for reassurance.
41. The 'structure' of your talk is the clarity and order of its presentation.
42. Self-assessment is crucial for setting new targets for improvement and achieving them.

Writing and The Media

1. Writing.
2. Around 1000 words.
3. Story line.
4. Kind of writing. For example, detective or horror stories.

5. The use 'as' or 'like' in the comparison.
6. An interesting beginning which draws the reader in.
7. The setting is where the story is supposed to be in time and place.
8. Check your answer with 'What You Can Write About' on page 31.
9. Writing that you have created yourself.
10. First and third person.
11. Third person.
12. The plan or outline of the story.
13. Notes, brainstorm or mind-map.
14. Fluency of expression and punctuation
15. Linear is a 'straight line'. There is no going backwards or forwards as the story unfolds. For example, *Romeo and Juliet* is a linear play because the action takes place over four days.

Personal Writing: Non-Fiction

16. Not made up.
17. Check your answer with 'What You Can Write About' on page 34. Any similar matches will be fine.
18. It means 'to ramble'. You could write about anything.
19. You can get information from knowledgeable people, libraries, the Internet, encyclopedias, companies, embassies, etc.
20. No.
21. The intended audience. Some authors target their novels at early readers; others go for the 10- to 14-year-old market.
22. Newspaper and magazine articles, leaflets, advertising posters, letters, petitions, proclamations, essays, reviews, etc. Anything like these would be fine.
23. Any piece of writing.
24. Instructions for: making a meal; finding directions to somewhere; putting a computer together; a booklet on how to keep fit, etc. Anything like this.
25. Yes.
26. To 'compare' is to examine what is similar; to 'contrast' is to say what is different.
27. The 'historical context' includes the events and ideas present at the time when the text was written or set.
28. You need a plan, an introduction, main body and a conclusion. It helps if you have a consistent argument too.
29. At the end of your essay.
30. This is essay technique: you make a 'point', give some appropriate 'evidence' for your point and 'comment', if you can do so.

The Media

31. A number of industries which transmit or 'mediate' information or entertainment in one form or another. These include the cinema, television, radio, record

companies, advertising, the Internet, etc.
32. All possibilities are too numerous to mention. They range from writing a radio script, analysing an advert, reviewing a film, to producing promotional resources for a pop band. Use common sense for your mark.
33. a) illustrations of any kind.
b) a large-size newspaper such as *The Guardian*.
c) the design and look of the page
d) a photo showing the face and sometimes the shoulders
e) large adverts with illustrations
34. a) the name of the journalist
b) only one paper carries the story
c) an emotional story perhaps on success or tragedy
d) the main part of the story
e) the main story on the front page
35. Check your answer against 'A Framework for Looking at Texts' on page 39.
36. Check your answer with the 'Use of Language' on page 40. If your answer is credible give yourself a mark.
37. Usually a catchy line which promotes a product. For instance, BT's is: 'It's good to talk'.
38. They create logos to promote their company image. Logos enable them to be easily recognised by consumers.
39. Check your answers throughout against 'Presentation and Layout' on page 41.
40. 'You', 'Dear Homeowner' and 'Dear Friend'.

Shakespeare

The Shakespeare Assignment

1. Check 'What you may study' on page 48 for possible suggestions. You may study other Shakespeare plays.
2. Read passages for general understanding or the gist first; then read for deeper meaning.
3. Check your answer with 'What you have to do' on page 49. There are other possibilities too.
4. Words and phrases cited from the play (text) as evidence in your writing.
5. Yes.
6. People produce new readings and interpretations of texts according to ideas and values, considered to be important in their time.
7. Imagery and the use of alliteration, assonance, onomatopoeia, etc.
8. History, Tragedy and Comedy. There is a sub-genre: Tragi-comedy.
9. What was then thought about the principles underlying human conduct and nature; how people thought the world worked, beliefs, etc.
10. Poetic verse, blank verse and prose.

11. For the end of scenes and scenes of dramatic intensity.
12. To show dignified speech; speech that helps convey feeling and mood.

Structure and Themes
13. A sense of normality and order. 'All is well with the world'.
14. Problems are introduced and order begins to break down.
15. The point of highest dramatic intensity before the protagonist's fall.
16. Battles, unmasking, deaths, marriages etc.
17. Order is restored and the right people are back in control.
18. A central idea or ideas.
19. Check your answers with those in 'Some Themes, Ideas, or Messages which recur throughout the plays' on page 50. There are other themes.
20. Love, appearance and reality, good and evil, identity and disguise, etc.
21. A comic scene is followed by a serious scene.
22. This makes a scene appear even more intense or light-hearted because of the contrasting emotions of the previous scene.
23. Self-knowledge is the ability to see learn from your faults when others point them out to you. Characters who do so 'develop'.
24. Order – problems – chaos – climax – resolution with new order.

Imagery and Essay Plans
25. Any kind of imagery or decorative language with alliteration, etc.
26. A comparison using 'as' or 'like'. For Instance, 'Clare is like a flower'.
27. It is a comparison which implies or states that something is something else: 'Clare is a flower'.
28. A metaphor that runs or is 'extended' over several lines or a scene.
29. It means 'person-making'. It is powerful metaphor in which things or ideas are given human traits for an enhanced literary effect.
30. Two opposite nouns yoked together for effect: 'A Hard Day's Night'.
31. A character, theme or image that recurs.
32. Imagery helps say more about points made in dialogue and action. It reinforces and enhances the audience's ideas of the characters. It can magnify or draw attention to themes/issues in the text.
33. Characters speak with irony when they say something that is truer than they realise.
34. It is dramatically ironic when the audience knows something important that characters do not. Sometimes this is complicated by one character knowing what another does with the audience sharing their knowledge.

35. Passages and scenes of dramatic intensity. An example is where Romeo first speaks with Juliet.
36. It includes figurative language, including word-pictures like similes and metaphors.

Poetry
How to Read and Study Poetry
1. 15%.
2. Reading.
3. Free-verse, quatrains, couplets, sonnets, etc.
4. At least three.
5. The attitude of the narrator to his or her topic and to the reader.
6. First and third person.
7. True.
8. A key message or idea.
9. False. It is a stanza.
10. False. You need to compare two or more poems or texts.
11. False. It is a simile.
12. Read and re-read for first impressions; read and re-read for meaning; sum up your final understanding of the poem.

How to Write About Poems
13. Two or more. Do not write about too many as your comments could be too thinly stretched.
14. A run-on line. Poets use them for effect.
15. To 'compare' is to note what is 'similar'; to 'contrast' is to explain what is different.
16. A figure of speech and a paradox in which two contradictory terms are brought together for an effect: 'awfully nice' and 'alone together'.
17. Usually mixed feelings or a paradox.
18. True. They are composed of two couplets.
19. Stanzas of irregular length and number.
20. It is an ideal form for conversation and argument.
21. Repetition of vowel sounds for an effect.
22. To make readers pause for reflection and emphasis; caesuras can add meaning to poems.
23. At the end of your essay. Do give your views because examiners are interested in what you think.
24. Make a few points well. If you have bullet points to guide you, you may not use them all.If you run out of time indicate, where you can, what you would say if you had the time.

Texts from Other Cultures and Traditions
25. These are texts written by speakers of English. The poets and writers use either local dialect or standard English in their texts and they mostly come from parts of the world where Britain once had a colonial influence.
26. Free-verse.
27. Glaswegian and West Indian. You could, of course, mention dialects from any part of the world that are part of the English language.

28. Check what you have studied with the syllabus of your exam board. The *NEAB Anthology* concentrates only on poetry with 'Poems from Other Cultures and Traditions'. Several of the other exam boards include short stories as well as poems.
29. Check your answers against the information on page 68.
30. Comment on it.
31. True.
32. True.
33. Free verse is the most natural form for conversation and argument.
34. John Agard thinks that the unthinking use of the terms and phrases such as 'half-caste' can lead to a racist viewpoint of seeing people of mixed race as only half human and unworthy of being treated as equals.
35. Half an hour.
36. Most of them. If you are with another exam board, do any of the themes mentioned in 'Finding Links between the Poems' on page 68 apply to your texts? Try to make a couple of connections and give yourself a mark.

Novels and Short Stories
How to Study Novels and Short Stories
1. Poems, short stories, plays and novels.
2. 1914 or before and it must be in prose.
3. It should be by an author named in the National Curriculum.
4. The time and events which took place when it was written.
5. Reading. However, you will need good writing skills to show your understanding.
6. The outline or structure of a piece of writing.
7. To explain what is different.
8. This refers to the kind or type of writing. For example, romance, adventure, detective, horror, etc.
9. How the writer creates effects through emotive or figurative writing.
10. Saying one thing while meaning another. Also speaking the truth without knowing it.
11. Connectives which allow you to move from one argument or point to another in a fluent manner. They are often key words or phrases that are needed at the beginning of paragraphs such as 'similarly' or 'on the other hand'.
12. Anything from 'Possible Assignments' on page 75 would do for this answer. Anything sensible will be good enough for a mark.

Literary Technique: Narrators, Characterisation and Dialogue
13. First and third person.
14. He or she uses 'I' because they are in the story.
15. Not necessarily. Do not confuse author with narrator.
16. Usually the third person. You can have a third-person omniscient all-seeing narrator.

17. Any of the ways set out on 'What to Look for in Characters' on page 76 will do for this answer.
18. The name of the main character is the name of the novel or story. For instance, Jane Austen's *Emma*.
19. Round characters develop because they change in the course of the novel. Flat characters do not change, thus they do not develop.
20. 'Conversation'. Two people speaking.
21. Dialogue makes characters vivid and lifelike. What characters say reveal their motives and personality traits; readers can learn about characters from what other characters say about them.
22. New speaker, new line and indent; begin with a capital letter; introduce with a punctuation mark and use inverted commas.
23. A character speaking alone.
24. The answer is similar to question 21. Look at the last two points of the answer to question 21.

Themes, Atmosphere and the Differences between Novels and Stories
25. Both have: plots, stories, dialogue, characters, themes and ideas.
26. Stories are shorter and tend to concentrate on an incident and have a shorter time-span for the action; there are also fewer characters with less detail; short stories tend to have one plot and fewer themes. Their dialogue is more fragmented. Description in short stories is more economical.
27. There is not enough space to do otherwise.
28. Through description; the use of imagery; through variety in language and sentences and through the tone of the narrator and his or her closeness to the action.
29. The choice of words chosen by the author.
30. True.
31. True.
32. False.
33. Alliteration is the repetition of initial consonants in words for an effect; assonance is the repetition of similar vowel sounds in words for an effect.
34. The main idea or message of a story.
35. Any sensible idea will be good enough here. Look again at 'Themes' on page 78 to see an example with *Roll of Thunder Hear My Cry*.
36. Check your answer by comparing novels and stories on pages 79. If you've mentioned a few of them give yourself the mark.

INDEX